the
small
church
VALID
VITAL
VICTORIOUS

the
small
church

VALID
VITAL
VICTORIOUS

PAUL O. MADSEN

JUDSON PRESS, VALLEY FORGE

THE SMALL CHURCH—VALID, VITAL, VICTORIOUS

Copyright © 1975
Judson Press, Valley Forge, PA 19481

Unless otherwise indicated, Bible quotations in this volume are in accordance with the Revised Standard Version of the Bible, copyrighted 1952 and 1971 by the Division of Christian Education of the National Council of the Churches of Christ in the United States of America, and are used by permission.

Bible quotations marked KJV are taken from *The Holy Bible,* King James Version.

Library of Congress Cataloging in Publication Data

Madsen, Paul O.
  The small church—valid, vital, victorious.

  Includes bibliographical references.
  1. Small churches. I. Title.
BV637.8.M32   254   74-22519
ISBN 0-8170-0669-9

Printed in the U.S.A.

Dedicated
to Shirley,
whose supportive spirit
has enriched my life.

CONTENTS

INTRODUCTION

One of the by-products of our American culture is that we are concerned with "bigness" and growth. A common assumption is that to be small is somehow wrong. The religious community has been affected by this secular attitude. Members in small churches frequently feel forgotten and neglected. When they seek help from the printed page, they find a very small library upon which to draw. Many of the books are quite old, oriented to a world moving at a much slower pace and, quite literally, a different culture. Very little has been published in this field since the close of World War II.

The author has had thirteen years of pastoral experience. Nine of those years were spent in a small church or in close fellowship and proximity to churches of less than one hundred members. More than twenty years have now been spent in the field of home missions, much of it directly related to the small church. There is a deep conviction that the small church is needed. It can be vital. It can make a difference in the individual and in the community. In many areas there is no option for ministry except through the small church. But there are more valid reasons than geographical necessity. The small church, historically, has moved the Christian cause forward. Because of its strong fellowship, ease of adaptability, and fast communication and mobilization, the small church is ideally suited for quick response to emerging needs. The faithfulness of members of the small church has provided inspiration to thousands in each decade. There is emotional warmth when one thinks of a small church with its close fellowship. These are values that are increasingly significant (and more difficult to keep) in our mass society.

Many small churches are not "small" in spirit. A part of the thesis of this book is that in a space and computer age, where miniaturization has become so critical, a church need not be big in numbers to discharge its mission faithfully. Why do twentieth-century Christians miss the lesson of the mustard seed that Jesus used? Perhaps the reason is that our urbanized culture would prevent most of us from recognizing a mustard seed if we saw one, unless it were encased in plastic and labeled as a good-luck charm.

The thoughtful reader will be asking, "Who decided the size of a small church?" There is no common definition between denominations. Some say the figure of 250, even 300, and some say 150. Somewhat arbitrarily, this book is using 200 as the dividing point. The rest of the book will reveal deviations from this figure that will prove its artificial character. However, in many denominational and interdenominational conferences, church leaders have concluded that any church of less than 200 is marginal. Such a church will have difficulty in adequately supporting its minister, providing essential maintenance of physical property, and carrying on an educational program. Very little will be left for mission in the community or in the world. The church will be forced to turn inward simply because the fight to survive will absorb the energies, the financial resources, and the time of the members. Christian theology is an outward-looking, sending theology. What then are we to do about structure, committees, and organization?

Advertising pressures us to "get more for our money." We may not really want more. In fact in some instances we might prefer less if we could get good quality, but planned obsolescence is not interested in quality, only in more production, more sales, more dollars.

Our cultural value structure is increasingly in conflict with our Christian value structure. What pastor of a small church has not felt slightly apologetic if in a ministers' meeting he must indicate the size of his church or congregation? The denomination, all too frequently, prepares its programs with elaborate committee structures, quite unmindful that such programs are manageable for perhaps one-third of all churches—the largest! Growth, for Christians, ideally is in both quality and quantity. Vital ministry, if forced to choose, must first be concerned with the spiritual values of life.

The United States as a whole is growing. However, many areas of our nation are not growing. In fact, many are declining in population. How does a church minister if the cultural impact, the denominational programming, yes, even the ministerial training, are oriented toward large churches in urban settings? Oddly enough, the casual observer would not immediately recognize that not all urban churches are large and successful. Again our culture assumes that everything in the city is large. Blighted areas of housing, industrialization, and expressway development isolate churches in pockets. A ministry may be even more desperately needed in such situations than elsewhere, but little growth in numbers can be anticipated.

How then can a spirit of mission be rekindled in such situations? What happens in an agricultural community that has been left to die slowly because modern farm machinery demands large acreages? How does a church minister in a community that once was a thriving community on a strong rail line, but now sees only one train a day going through, if that? The community economy has changed because of the ubiquitous motorcar and highway truck, and stores now stand empty. What of the great mother church of the metropolis that has an auditorium for two thousand—now closed—and a chapel seating two hundred that has plenty of seats left on Sunday morning at 11 A.M., and now is faced with problems of being too small?

Is there hope? Are there answers, or if not answers, directions? Can a church be faithful in mission if it does not always follow all denominational procedures that call for such an organization that it could not even fill the committees, much less do the work? It is commonly said that most churches spend 90 percent of their energies on housekeeping chores related to internal structures and 10 percent on mission. Can this be reversed? Will denominational and interdenominational offices really care? Will people take heart? Many remain faithful but discouraged. Can this tide be reversed?

The author has a deep conviction that the body of concerned people is larger than has been realized. If this book, in its effort to answer some of the foregoing questions, does no more than unite some of those who share the challenge of the ideas expressed here, the author will be satisfied. What seems to be needed at this point is not agreement on techniques, but rather a disciplined corps of concerned people who recognize the value and more—the continuing need—for the small church in modern America. If this book can augment the concerned group now in existence, focus discussion, and bring action, then the hours of labor will have been well spent. Agreement on procedures is not necessarily desired, although, obviously, the author's ego would respond to such.

Far more critical is the need for thoughtful planning in order that the children of this day, wherever they may live, may hear the Good News. The parable of the lost sheep still has relevance. In a mass society, the Christian message is concerned, of course, for society and its needs, for man does not live alone. But God's love still belongs to the least also. We can and do rejoice in numbers, but we cannot forget that the message belongs to all, individually, wherever they may live, however isolated they may be.

The small church has a place in the mission task that can be filled by no other group. It must be encouraged and it must be strengthened. It must be given the recognition and status which rightfully belong to it as a partner in mission.

I am bewildered as I try to find a way to express appreciation to the many who encouraged me in the various stages of writing and who responded to my entreaties for information about statistics and outstanding case histories. Their enthusiasm and concern for the small church gave encouragement to me in some moments when encouragement was needed. To the scores who responded and to some of whom will find their material omitted because of space requirements, I can only voice my thanks in this all too slight a way. I am grateful to Karin Szerenyi for work on the manuscript and especially to Doris Mitchell, who began as a typist, then became secretary, and has become a friend and colleague through projects such as this book, and I am in her debt above all others.

Paul O. Madsen

Chapter

1

WHAT IS
A
SMALL CHURCH?

In the world in which we live, the adjective "small" carries a negative connotation for many. In days of burgeoning population, fantastic exploration into space, high-speed jet travel, and other similar events, "smallness" is a term to be avoided. In the pages of literature, a "small man" is one of low ideals, cunning, and perhaps deceitful ways, a man to be viewed with suspicion. Thus, one seems to speak of stigma, defeat, and guilt if one uses the term "the small church."

Yet "small" has positive values, too. Insurance companies recognize a "compact car" and adjust insurance rates. Space exploration has been made possible because scientists have been zealous in making motors, radios, and guidance equipment smaller and smaller. Miniaturization and solid-state circuitry are well established in industry and have led to more comfort and convenience in the home, in the car, and in the office, through application. Air conditioners are less bulky. Refrigerators of the same size have more space for food because of "miniaturization."

It would appear that the value that is put into the word "small" depends upon what it is used to modify.

A Definition

What do we mean when we say "small church"?

Most church people would say that a church of 150 members or less is a small church. Others would say that a church of 200 is in this classification, and still others, one of 250. Regardless of the number, a small membership means a church that is hard pressed to maintain an organization and committee structure that permits it to participate fully, completely, and in a satisfying way in the life of the denomination and the community. Such a church will have an inadequate budget in most instances, which in turn may lead to a high rate of turnover in pastors. Even if a pastor were content to accept the salary that would be offered, he or she still would not be content to accept the limited program of service and ministry that would be possible on a starvation budget. Size is not the only criterion, however.

A definition must be concerned with quality as well as quantity in ministry. Even as some small things in our world are to be sought, so there are qualities in a small church that should be cherished. The small church can be quick in response, for membership can be mobilized more easily. Participation and involvement is usually at a higher ratio. It can be flexible in approach, for communication is faster and involves fewer channels. An army traditionally sends out scouts to chart the territory, find the obstacles, and report recommended procedures. Small churches, whether in the city or town or country, are admirably suited for such a role. They are usually in a more threatened position, caused by changes in society. Because they are located in places of stress and change, new programs and methods can be tested in such situations. Members of a small church are often more sensitive to immediate problems around them and are eager for guidance, for their lives are more visibly threatened. The fellowship in a small church can be rich and meaningful, for people are able to take a keener interest simply because their lives are intertwined on a continuing basis rather than an irregular one as is often the case in a large church. Members of small churches are usually better contributors, per capita, than members of large churches. The intimacy of close fellowship can be helpful in evangelism. These assets are too valuable to be ignored or neglected.

Smallness does not mean lack of faithfulness on the part of the church members, nor of the congregation as a unit. It does not have to mean lack of efficiency either. Later, there will be illustrations of churches of less than two hundred members that have significant ministries that are creative and satisfying to the church, to its members, and to the community which the church serves. A member of a small church may actually find that spiritual values are more easily obtained than in a large church. The fellowship can be richer because of less internal organizational structure. People are known individually and recognized as persons. There is community. Smallness can mean that time-consuming and often abortive administrative chores are stripped away. Essentials have to be nearer the heart of the program. Lack of attention to essentials becomes apparent much more quickly. The core is too near the surface for any rot to be hidden for long. It may be ignored, but it cannot be hidden.

The concept of "smallness" with its negative image may be forced upon many of today's churches by the denomination and its patterns. Lay persons should be persistent in indicating areas where small churches seem to be ignored, slighted, or left in the position of seemingly not being wanted. In most denominations, program and planning are based upon a certain committee structure that is considered basic. This structure will often be well in excess of one hundred persons for all boards and committees if the traditional denominational approaches, as such, are to be maintained. A small church of two hundred that has the national average of 20 percent nonresident members and another 20 percent inactive is perilously near the minimum requirement for maintaining committees, even if it enlists everyone. In the so-called active congregation, there will be those who, because of health, age, or other factors, can do little beyond attending worship and sharing in only the most limited way.

A church can usually count on about 40 percent of the membership for any active, ongoing participation in the life of the church. If a denomination sets up structure that requires 100 or more persons for leadership, a church has to have at least 250 members to meet this criterion. No wonder there is often a feeling of guilt in the lives of individual church members when a new brochure arrives calling for a new program. The individual church member may already be singing in the choir, serving on a board and several sub-committees, teaching in the Sunday school, helping with the youth program, and trying to be at least a member of a men's or women's group. The church and the person are overorganized, and guilt feelings are a result. The denominations themselves force the concept of smallness on a church all too often and breed, by promotional pressure, the feeling of inadequacy and negativism.

This pressure, in turn, may come in measure from the secular culture of our day. The often discussed "Madison Avenue techniques" of promotion, success stories, affluent congregations, and beautiful buildings create another unrecognized pressure on a small church. The small business concerns, especially those run by "Mom and Pop," are in serious difficulty today. Small manufacturing companies often merge to seek diversification, reduced costs, and more maneuverability in order to be able to compete. Many small towns are dying or declining in size. The witness of the secular world is that if an organization is to be counted as successful, it must be at least big enough to have extra energy and resources that can be used for more than simply staying alive.

Quite obviously, from a religious-value standard, there is need for a qualitative measurement of the life of the church as well as for a quantitative method. The Bible either has significant eternal truths or else it does not. One does not go far before one reads of Gideon reducing his forces to become effective. Jesus had only twelve disciples. Paul depended upon the support of only a handful as he went from place to place in his missionary journeys. The history of the Christian advance is based upon the few who caught the vision and moved forward. They were not dismayed because their immediate group was small and the world was large. The test for Christian people must still be based upon effectiveness and faithfulness rather than upon size and success as the world measures. Quality of living still has significance, even in the twentieth century.

Denominations have all too often done their planning for the larger churches. This cannot continue. In the changing patterns of population of today, there are greater numbers of people who are often caught in situations of static or declining communities. They still need a ministry. Furthermore, the major denominations have, on the average, some 40 percent of their churches in the category of 150 members or fewer. The United Methodists, alone, for example, have 64 percent (25,095) of their churches under 200 in size.

Reasons for Size

It obviously would be wise to do some analysis of why churches are small, if any planning is to be done for a faithful ministry and realistic participation by small churches. These situations may well provide problems or opportunity for future ministry.

An Inadequate Program

Some churches remain small because of the limited program that is offered. People's needs are not met. An adequate church should provide Christian education on a sustained basis. It does not have to be completely graded but should have enough divisions to keep those in attendance in an age and interest group that matches their development. The church should have a regular program of evangelism that is broader than the traditional preaching mission. Lay persons should be involved in calling for new converts, conservation of new members, and maintenance of fellowship among all of the congregation. This is essential not simply for the perpetuation of the church as institution but also for the nurture and fulfillment of the individual Christian. A part of our theology is concerned with the joyous sharing of one's faith. Not to have that opportunity is a denial to the individual of a major source of fulfillment in one's own faith. There should be regular opportunity for Bible study. This may be in several homes simultaneously to avoid the stereotype and familiarity of the midweek service. Groups can easily be led by lay persons who have prepared themselves for such leadership. There should be opportunity for members of the church who are concerned about social issues and other special interests to be involved in such problems, with knowledge, support, and sponsorship of the church. There should be regular opportunities for worship, though this does not always have to be under the leadership of an ordained minister. There must also be consistent involvement in the wider outreach of the church, through denominational mission programs, ecumenical study, and participation. Any less than the above would be a program that would be inadequate in providing an individual with the necessary spiritual environment for personal growth.

An Inadequate Field

Some churches have an inadequate field due to the fact that an interstate highway has bisected the community, effectively cutting off a large segment of the population in such a way that they literally cannot get to church without long and difficult travel. Persons in urban areas can be expected to travel about twenty minutes at the most if their participation in the life of the church is to be maintained at a satisfactory level. For a church to fight to maintain membership beyond that time limit is unrealistic. There is simply too much energy and time involved, particularly if families are considered. If there is little population within that time circle or if several churches are competing, then it is poor Christian stewardship to attempt to maintain the ministry as is.

A church may have been founded to minister to a particular language or ethnic group and been tardy in the recognition of the decline in the group to which it was ministering. In urban areas, the shift in cultural and racial groups has been dramatic and swift. Many churches have been unable to shift as rapidly and have lost ground. Members move into another community but keep the church tie for a while, resisting the newcomer who is now in the church neighborhood. Often there is direct and obvious resistance to racial integration. At best there is slowness of response and inability to understand the need for an openness or a change in some worship and fellowship patterns. The church should not fight sociological change. There is nothing unchristian in such recognition. If scriptural support is needed, Paul recognized the culture of the people to whom he preached and sought to reach them at the level of their understanding and living.

It may be that in a rural area, a town that was once a major railroad junction has seen the railroad cease operation, and the town's young people move away. The population of the community may be cut in half, but the number of churches remains the same. Usually, the number of churches, even at the population peak, was predicated upon a growing population. It may have been recognized that there were too many churches for the population at the date of founding, but "our town is going to grow." The reasons for the community disappeared, but the community didn't disappear and neither do the churches. In such instances, the community cannot sustain the churches. Consideration must be given to merger, relocation, or closing, for a program cannot be maintained under present circumstances.

In an urban area, what was once a residential community may have been rezoned. Business or light industry has moved in. There may have been a change in the basic economy, either in urban or town-and-country areas. There are only pockets of people left. This is a most perplexing problem, for the gospel is based upon the ministry to the individual. The parable of the lost sheep is often quoted. Yet the way to maintain a ministry in pockets is most difficult to find, for people are conditioned to a church building, a pastor, and a traditional program. They resist any change in these norms, even though they can neither afford nor support such norms. Actually, the denominations of today are wasting millions of dollars in maintaining expensive buildings often on valuable land. Great amounts of staff time are usually required simply because sentiment supersedes stewardship. Population shifts mean that reconsideration must be given. The Bureau of Census of the U.S. government has said, "Half of all the counties in the United States lost in population during this decade of record growths. Most of those losing population in 1960 also lost in the 1940–1950 decade. Of the rural counties (those with no population center of 2500 or more) 77 percent lost in population." This loss of population raises great problems for public and private institutions, for schools and for the churches. It becomes even more serious when one looks at who is leaving, since by and large the loss of population in these counties is in young people of working age.

Centralized schools, centralized markets, and all-weather roads have changed travel patterns and friendship ties in town-and-country areas. These changes sometimes threaten the local church's stability.

The military forces are grappling with the same problem, for modern warfare and defense require small units scattered over wide regions. The Armed Forces Chaplains Board is finding ways of maintaining a ministry, but it is not relying solely upon beautiful chapels, with services on Sunday morning. It does not wait upon tradition and for people to come at traditional times. It seeks the people. So must the civilian church.

Inadequate Evangelism

The line between an inadequate field and inadequate evangelism is a very fine line that is difficult to distinguish. A slothful congregation may claim an inadequate field as an excuse.

Long-time members of a congregation witness the gradual moving of fellow members; but they do not recognize that there may actually be more people in the community than ever before, for they are of a different background. There may be a racial change. One-family dwellings may have become rooming houses with a change in the economic class level. A farm area may have merged into a suburban bedroom community. The conservatism of long-term members often means that they overlook, ignore, or actually fear the newcomer group.

The new group represents a threat to them because new people will bring new ways. The patterns that have existed so long and have provided comfort will go. Many ministers move, not because of restlessness, dissatisfaction with salary, or housing arrangements, but because of the inertia of the members of the small church. The lack of willingness to change may mean a dull, caretaker ministry. A pastor with initiative cannot long endure such a situation. There may be a lack of knowledge of how to penetrate the community and evangelize the newcomer. But first and foremost is the willingness to undertake such a ministry. Techniques can be learned where vision is present.

There are other reasons, too, why a church will follow a program that is inadequate for evangelism and growth. It may be deceived by seeing the new members who are joining, but not recognize that these are coming by transfer. This is not evangelism, but is, more accurately, conservation. Even where there are baptisms, there needs to be some examination to determine if the baptisms are coming from families that are members of the church already or if the baptisms really represent new families. The breadth of the base is critical as well as the numbers who join.

Some new churches reach a "plateau" and do not grow beyond the small-church category. The reasons can be several, but often the cause is for the foregoing because they unconsciously rely upon transfers and baptisms of children in committed families and then suddenly become a little island in the new community. They have not really penetrated the community at all, but have simply appealed to the like-minded who were there. Evangelism authorities say that a newcomer who has not identified with a church in the first six months of residency is very difficult to reach after that time and usually will not identify with the church.

If there is a class culture, or race problem, or if there is a highly personalized viewpoint that centers on the individual rather than mutual concern in the church body, the church will have trouble. If there is self-reliance on the part of individuals rather than a feeling of collective concern and care for others, the church will experience difficulties.

An Inadequate Vision

When a church becomes a static church and remains on a plateau receiving just enough new members to balance the losses, are there identifiable reasons? Again, the list cannot be exhaustive at this point, but there are some reasons that need to be listed for further thought and study as these pages move along.

Reference has already been made to "pocket" communities, which are caused by new highways, urban redevelopment, and economic or sociological change. The church may not have developed methods to be kept informed of new residents through newcomer lists, new utility subscribers, and the like.

One of the most serious problems is that of the "over-churched" community. As has already been pointed out, this overchurching may have happened because it seemed that growth patterns would provide a constituency for the churches, but then the growth pattern changed.

Some denominational polities do not permit easy solving of this problem.

If local churches are autonomous, they can ignore sociological changes, basic Christian stewardship, and the image they project to the unevangelized to cling to their ways. In 1958 the National Council's Commission on Town and Country developed an excellent set of criteria for the churching of town-and-country communities. Those valuable standards are still waiting to be used. The urban and racial crises of the 1960s redirected energies and resources of staff to the seemingly more urgent priorities. Furthermore the planning involved in the criteria was excellent at a national level but did not involve denominational units and local church members in the process.

Cooperation on development of principles is quite different than cooperation in implementing those principles. Lay persons need to be involved in the development so that from the beginning the work will not be left to professionals. The knowledge that professionals can bring is excellent, provided there are previously established channels to distribute and use this knowledge. On the urban scene the lack of support for the town-and-country criteria has even prevented the development of comparable urban criteria, for the futility of the effort, to this date, is too easily observable. Hence, there are no ecumenical criteria for churching of urban communities.

A major denomination, through research, has found that a primary cause of churches being small lies in the simple fact that the churches are often not in growing places. In that denomination, one-third of the urban churches and almost 40 percent of the town-and-country churches are in static or declining communities. Many of those churches were founded to meet a particular need. The conditions have changed. The tragedy, however, is that even in these circumstances there are unchurched people in the community who are neglected. On a national average, roughly 40 percent of the population will have no church affiliation. Another 20 percent will be so nominally related that for all practical purposes they are unrelated. In some areas of our nation, particularly in the West, this percentage will be far higher.

To assume, therefore, that there is no opportunity for growth in a static or declining community is untrue. The task is more difficult. There will need to be a creative approach developed, for obviously the present program of the church is not appealing. It can be done, however, if there is vision.

One of the most distressing situations is the family chapel. The majority of the membership is interrelated because of long residency or national or ethnic background. It becomes a tight, little enclave, calling a pastor who virtually becomes a chaplain to the family. Any change in programming becomes especially difficult because of the "clan" and their feelings for each other.

Inadequate Personalities

Experiences are common to many of visiting "a cold church" or "a friendly church." These are not the only personality characteristics that exist in corporate personality of a local church. Some churches are notably outgoing, concerned about youth, involved in social issues, ministering to the aging. Others are identified by their "set" ways, their stingy attitudes, their suspicious nature, their "clannishness." Personalities belong to groups as well as individuals. There are factors that cause or inhibit personality growth in individuals, and these same factors move into all groups in social life as well, including the church. While this may seem less specific and less tangible than some of the preceding potential factors in smallness, it may be the most common and the most critical. It may also be the most difficult to change.

Some churches stop growing because their personalities are not winsome. They are not attractive to a newcomer or to a long-term resident. Sometimes that personality is shaped by ingrown leadership, both lay and clerical. Sometimes it is shaped by one individual who tries to dominate the church for ego satisfaction, finding in power in the church organization what cannot be achieved in the community, its lodges, organizations, and groups. Sometimes the church is captured by those who are concerned for "theological purity" and thus inhibit any questing spirit. On occasion there are churches that are dominated by long-term residents who have the finest of intentions but feel that any newcomer must wait five years before speaking. The members of many years "know what is best for the church and its people because we have been here longer." There are many reasons why it may be so, but it remains that many people prefer a church that is small and try to keep it that way. Some reasons are valid, for the people recognize the better record in evangelism, financial support, and fellowship that can be possible. Other reasons are far less valid. Individuals need to look at themselves and their fellow members to be quite certain that motivations for action are as they should be in Christian groups.

Paul writes in the New Testament of those who live on milk and those who are ready for meat. Some churches never move out of their infancy into maturity. They remain unpredictable, unstable on goals, and seem to be casting about for their role in mission in the community. To a certain extent they are churches which can become victims of penetration by sect groups which eventually remove the church from its denominational ties. They have not yet matured in the Christian faith.

Small churches need to be vigilant, for they are more easily made into a victim for petty people and petty thinking. There are fewer people to combat an overly aggressive personality. One person can more easily dominate several areas than in larger churches, where boards are likely to be larger and where there is more internal organization with checks and balances.

Psychological pressures, therefore, may well carry more weight in a small church and may help to keep it small, as they shape the church in its character, personality, and program. The feelings of inadequacy, guilt, and resignation that often exist in the small church vitiate the finest of efforts often before those efforts have gotten under way.

This effect is compounded if the community is undergoing severe change because of economic, sociological, or other reasons. Those things which have usually been dependable in community life vanish. Stability is torn away from individuals, and the church becomes a refuge. The reason may not be recognized, but serious efforts are made to keep the church the same, for it is the last remnant of a world that was. The church can be more easily controlled in its program than can government, civic agencies, and other forms of community organization. If people are threatened by outward change, the church represents a place where they turn for refuge and lack of change. The old hymns, familiar building, and the traditional form of services give a feeling of security in a changing world, but they also can lead to a static or dying church.

More Than Adequacy

The previous headings have used the word "inadequate." It is one of the failures of the English language that sometimes the opposite of a word does not carry the opposite value.

To write this book on the adequate church would be a minimizing of the power of the gospel, a demeaning of the reader, and an injustice to many small churches that are or can be engaged in far more than just an adequate ministry. That would be settling for too little—for crumbs when a loaf is available.

Three words will show up throughout this book—valid, vital, and victorious. They are not here simply for alliteration, but because of their centrality in Christian theology and experience.

> There are valid ministries to be performed.
> They are vital for persons who need the
>   ministry and for those who offer it.
> They can be victorious for the individual,
>   the church, and the cause of Jesus Christ.

Brief references have been made to some of the values that can be found in the small church. Obviously, the writing of this book would not have been undertaken if there were no values in the small church or reasons for it to be maintained.

To let that stand, however, as a casual assumption with only brief reference or peripheral attention would be unfair and misleading.

Not all churches should be large, even if there were the opportunity for them to be. It needs to be very quickly added that no such statement should be used as an excuse for inadequate vision, evangelism, or programming. If a church elects to be small, it should know clearly why it is doing so.

Validation for Small Churches

A church may accept smallness, given the geographical area in which it works, but then resolve to move into a rounded program that is satisfying and fulfilling to the individual members. The acceptance of reality may prove to be the stepping stone to a renewed or changed vision of what ministry can be. Some of the case histories in this manuscript have come about at exactly that point. Churches have looked at the potential for growth and have seen some, but have recognized that there are limits. Having accepted those limits, they have come to a psychologically sound position of acceptance of themselves. Happiness is often based on such acceptance, and unhappiness comes in the wistfulness of wishing for what cannot be.

Some churches have chosen a style of ministry that they feel is needed and essential but which is less popular among the rank and file of potential church members. Sometimes the discipline that is demanded in financial support, or personal participation, is higher than many individuals are prepared to share.

Still other churches have deliberately set their feet upon a pathway that for many years will keep them small. They may be seeking to be a "bridge" church between racial or economic or cultural groups. This relatively unpopular task which is most essential is less appealing. Other churches have found specific needs and have made their appeals consciously to a ministry for the aging or a national or an ethnic group, or a specialized ministry such as to the deaf.

These churches are to be honored, for they have accepted a responsibility which they are more than willing to discharge even though it means they will remain among the smaller churches.

The joy of the Christian church is in faithfulness in mission. To set a goal and move toward that goal is the highest victory in the Christian faith.

Saul was on the road to Damascus when he had a spiritual experience that literally turned him around in the road and reversed his goals in life.

Many small churches need to have that kind of experience of reversing their viewpoints. For many reasons there have been negativism, pessimism, a feeling of futility, and other similar feelings. These have come often because a church has looked at itself on the basis of the single standard of growth in numbers. The Damascus experience for Paul was in seeing a new standard of judgment for his life. The small church often needs to find a new standard for its life, in a full spiritual ministry to all who live within its shadow.

A part of the turning-around experience is recognizing the assets which a small church has:

- Warmth and intimacy of fellowship, which a large church has to work to achieve but which is more natural to a small church;
- The possibility of identifying mission and concentrating upon it;
- The ability to be more flexible in approach, to minimize structure and to reach agreement more easily.

There are many outstanding examples of vital small churches across our nation in all denominations. Many religious communities that have emphasized service and ministry have also accepted a smaller size as being not merely a condition but as an actual asset to be used. The Society of Friends and the Church of the Brethren leap quickly to mind as two national groups that have been dedicated and have used small size as an asset in mobility and mission. There are many small congregations that have done the same that have been written up in the popular press. This book will add still other instances to that collection. These congregations are not only vital in their ministry but also have proved the validity of the ministry and thus have become victorious in the fullest sense of Christian theology, for they have found life in being willing to surrender it.

In the past, there have been people of great achievement who have come from small churches. The trend is changing, but at one time these churches produced the majority of ministers and missionary candidates. Until a few short years ago, the bulk of leaders of urban churches traced their beginnings to small churches, often in town and country. The small church, at its best, has inherent values for producing the kind of atmosphere that stimulates and nourishes a person in spiritual development. With the thousands of churches in our nation in this "small church" classification, and because of what they can mean for the total Christian enterprise, the potential cannot be neglected.

Perhaps the most vital asset that is needed is the courage to be small. The pages of history are filled with persons who should have given up because of their physical stature. They did not. Modern science is spending millions of dollars in research, questing for ways to make things smaller for the future welfare of mankind. The small church is not an anachronism. It has a place and that place is a vital one.

If the modern church, through its denominational and interdenominational structures, and through its regional and national bodies, will make a conscious decision to assist the small church, then the tide can be turned. At the moment, there are few friends, a great deal of neglect, and too little attention at the critical points of program that will turn the church outward in service.

Consecrated leadership, convinced of the values that can still be found in the small things of life, for example, the mustard seed or grain of wheat, can communicate a courage to thousands who are waiting for their opportunity to serve faithfully in the kingdom.

Chapter

2

SOME PROBLEMS
AND
SOLUTIONS

Many small churches are struggling. They seek for a minister more often than large churches do, for the rate of movement in the small-church clergy is approximately twice that of churches in general. The budget is chronically in jeopardy. There are perennial building problems particularly with small urban churches. There is a feeling of guilt over denominational mail, with new programs, which remains unanswered or answered with a "no." Leadership is overburdened. Problems are always present.

Frequently the people of the church find themselves in a compound problem as they may live in a changing inner-city neighborhood or in a small town which is static or declining. The same problems which are in the church are in the community, and each affects the other.

Pessimism is difficult to dispel under such circumstances, for in the home, church, and community, there are the same factors of despair. Energies are dissipated and hope dies, for there is too little success in any area. Defeat is too common. This is not true of all small churches and the communities that surround them, but it is general enough that it becomes a vital factor which must be faced by all in planning positions. The church, which is supposed to be the harbinger of hope, is itself a victim of hopelessness.

The quantitative problems of budget, small membership, and lack of leadership are difficult. The qualitative problems of incomplete program, long-range planning, and inhibited leadership are more debilitating spiritually and breed a psychological attitude that is often self-defeating. The people begin to feel they are on the margins of life instead of being a part of the center.

Psychological Attitudes

The church often turns inward in such situations in an attempt to perpetuate itself. It thus increases its own problem because it has no energy or time for evangelism, social action, and community interest. It becomes a tight, little enclave which seeks desperately, or even worse, seeks haphazardly for solutions to institutional problems of budget, leadership, and program. The focus is wrong. Theologically, the church should be turned outward. Its concern must always be for the world created by God. But in its own illness, it is struggling to keep the lifeblood moving within its own body and has no strength left for those outside its own small body. It has not learned the spiritual truth that Jesus enunciated so long ago, "that he who would find his life must lose it." The church struggles instead to preserve its own life and in the end may die, for its focus has become material and not spiritual.

Smallness has been a subject of study by competent authorities for many decades. In religious life as well as physical life, smallness can become a severe psychological handicap when the assumption is made that physical growth and bigness are the correct goals. If the denomination orients itself to such a concept and lets this attitude permeate all of its literature, teaching materials, program, and promotional aids, then a small church is under an almost impossible burden. Smallness is also a deterrent when the denomination assumes that all churches must have a full program but does not carefully spell out what this "full program" may mean for churches both above and below the average size in terms of full participation by each.

The small church is further handicapped because it is fighting for its status and role in the life of the community. If it has no observable function and remains as a peripheral organization, certainly those who are outside will find little incentive to join. The people of the church may feel that they know the role and function of the church in the community, and it may be that they do, intellectually. However, until they begin to express it in everyday concern, they will not succeed in being winsome enough to bring new vitality to their corporate life. It is tragic but true that in our day much of the original program of the church is now being performed by other groups in the community. There will be groups which give fellowship. There will be organizations formed for some aspect of civic betterment that will carry the social-concern function. If a special need arises, a new group may be created in the community which may include a member of the clergy but will normally be outside the religious community, identified as such. The church thus loses relevance. It is known to exist. It may preserve the function of providing a personal religion, but this is inadequate for a rounded ministry and meaningless to the community as such. Secular members of the community recognize the church building when they pass by. They will remember it on Sundays, even though they do not attend, for they may hear a churchly reference on the radio or be reminded of the church simply in the absence of the usual workday schedule or by hearing the bell. But the comprehensive role and function of the church will remain unknown to the people of the community until the church turns outward in ministry and service.

When such a pattern begins to emerge, it is a descending spiral that becomes most difficult to reverse. The lack of true identification with community needs leads to a kind of incestuous relationship within the church, for the people are dependent upon each other. Tradition begins to be the dominant force even though the Christian faith has always made its greatest impact when it has been untraditional. It is easier to keep on doing what has been done rather than to make the effort to change. Human nature all too often accepts the present reality, even though unsatisfying, instead of going on a crusade, however modest, for a change in direction. The status quo is always more comfortable, simply because it consumes less energy. It is not a conscious rigidity that sets in, for most persons would instinctively not like to see themselves classified in that way.

In a recent study in one denomination, more than 60 percent of all churches were involved in "conventional" programs, but the percentage of conventionality was much higher in the smaller churches. It is almost a paradox that a small church can move more easily because of the fewer persons who are involved, but is also harder to move because the deviations from the norm find less acceptability. In a larger group, there is room for a greater range of groups and clusters of like-minded people, and the "odd" person is more apt to find a kindred spirit simply because there is more variety of thought.

In any setting today the conventional program in an individual congregation is in trouble. There is too much ferment among women, youth, and racial and cultural groups for patterns of the past. In every church, large or small, there is a need for a rethinking of the role and mission of the church. Form is not the issue but mission is. People are hurting, and those hurts need "the balm of Gilead" in all of its infinite variety. To minister in ritualistic ways that were appealing in another generation means an almost automatic rejection by the present generation. Many persons may rebel at the rewriting of the hymns of the past by the women's lib movement as they remove all "men." However, any church that seeks to speak today will have to face that issue somehow even if it takes a less radical stand than eliminating hymns that refer to "the men of God." This kind of instance can be duplicated in many realms. Tradition and conventionality have been found wanting by much of the world of today. A revolution is taking place in value standards and in the way that people live and think. The church must understand and accept those persons as people even if their value patterns are not accepted. To reject blindly without critical examination and possible modification of one's own patterns means isolation and inevitable death.

How does a church accept a community and yet maintain its own Christian identity? Judson Memorial Church, of Greenwich Village, New York City, is an example of such a church. Though it has an identifiable community, it also has a widely dispersed membership. It has opportunity for a vital ministry in the surrounding community through mobilizing its resources and channeling its energies to those problems. It has abandoned many of the traditional boards and committees of the church as being time-consuming and frustrating to what it regards as its central mission. The church has about one hundred members and is identified with the American Baptist Churches and the United Church of Christ. Howard Moody and Al Carmines have given outstanding pastoral leadership. Its ministry has been criticized at times because of the church's willingness to take risks in order to be involved with those who surround its doors. While it is well located on the edge of a park and is easily seen, it has not rested in that visibility. It has felt that it must reach out and not be content to assume that those who pass by will come in. The staff of the church has been encouraged to participate in various aspects of community life, including direct political action, civil-rights activities, and involvement with juveniles caught in the throes of drug addiction. Located in a community of artists, the church has loaned its facilities for concerts and exhibits which on occasion have offended the traditionalists. The church, however, has felt that it must be alert to those who live within its shadows and understand their thoughts and their modes of living and of expression. It has found vitality and witness by being a ministering church through visionary leadership that looks at service as being primary. It has thoughtfully defined its mission and moves conscientiously in meeting that mission.

The people of God must be open. The Israelites had problems in believing God about the Promised Land. A return to the captivity of yesterday looked more attractive than the unknown land of milk and honey. The tragedy of the Exodus from Egypt was that the people who followed Moses began to make and worship their own gods and thus wandered in the wilderness for forty years, spiritually bereft until a new generation grew up. The analogy is an apt one in the day in which we live, for in large measure we, too, have created false gods of conformity, reference to the past, and comfort in the established way of other years. We, too, have preferred our slavery of the past even though our faith bids us move forward in the promise of God. Structure is not sacred. It is necessary, but when current structure gets in the way of mission, evangelism, stewardship, and other

Christian concerns, it is no longer a usable tool and must be changed.

Blind obedience to an eleven o'clock service on Sunday morning may be an anachronism that is self-defeating. The necessities of a dairy herd need no longer dictate the hour of worship. To insist on a paid clergyman, who may be ill trained and forced to supplement income by secular work, for the sake of tradition is of dubious value. Shared clergy may be better stewardship. Lay ministries can be spiritually rewarding and may be more relevant. To insist on holding a church school on Sunday morning, when teachers may be too few and too occupied with conflicting responsibilities in the home or the church choir, or some other aspect of living, is a denial of ministry. The pattern of activity in the church might be redesigned and scattered throughout the week so that full attention can be given, rather than crowding everything into a few brief hours on Sunday morning and putting people under tension because the clock will not permit so much activity in such a brief span of time.

In Baton Rouge, Louisiana, the Fellowship Baptist Church with ninety-four members has followed a different format in worship, organization, and procedure. The church began as an "independent" Baptist group wishing to be ecumenical in its stance. It has deliberately set forth on a pathway that it recognizes as being difficult and one that may keep it small. The congregation has a sincere belief, however, that it has a mission to be performed in its geographical setting and in its theological understanding. Partially as a result of this attitude, it has three types of constituency which it recognizes: directing members, supporting members, and participating members, with financial and spiritual commitment stipulated. It also has a structured trial membership "for those investigating. . . ." It is a part of the worship pattern of the church that there be a sermon-discussion period in order that the congregation may examine carefully and thoughtfully not only the content of the sermon but also its application in the lives of members. The church sponsors drama, art, and writing groups which it hopes will become a form of witness for the members of the church. The church also has what it calls "Growth Groups" meeting throughout the week, whose primary purpose is to provide for each member a personal experience in increasing Christian maturity. The extensive study groups are augmented by a large library of tapes that are circulated to supporting members who may live in other states.

Methodists owe much of their present-day strength to the old "class meetings" which were an antecedent of the modern, small face-to-face groups. This is a value which people still cherish and which is an incalculable asset that the small church may have. But in the blind aping of the large-church pattern of many Sunday activities, the asset is lost. Detailed study of small churches, such as Baton Rouge, that are effective reveals that consciously or unconsciously they have spread their programs over the week. They have allowed people time for preparation, participation, and fellowship with leisure and thus have become significant churches not only for the membership but also for the community. They have again discovered a function and a role that is a meaningful one for the people.

Small churches faced with short-term pastorates have too seldom given thoughtful attention to what they seek in a pastor. They settle for a preacher. Often they settle, too, for availability rather than precise skills which may be in keeping with the church's understanding of what it wants and needs. Actually, such an analysis of needs might lead to longer pastorates, for the minister and the church would have more goals in common. A good preacher is helpful as well as a person who will be an effective pastor. Most small churches, however, need a professional leader who will become an enabler, helping the people of the church to assume more responsibility and leadership. The clergy should not seek to do those things which can be handled as ably and perhaps even more so by the members of the congregation. There are many resident skills in lay persons which often lie neglected. A small church needs to encourage lay leaders "to try their wings" and in seeking a pastor should find one who sees as primary "equipping the saints" for their ministry.

The small church must understand itself and find that which will provide a feeling of satisfaction and accomplishment if there is to be spiritual health.

Significant encouragement is to be found in the establishment of a research center on the small church by McCormick Theological Seminary in Chicago. This is a comprehensive project analysis of effectiveness. The research will involve the various roles of the pastor, the characteristics of the small church, and the responsibility of the denominational unit in its work with the small church. After the research is completed, there will be movement toward a revitalization process involving delivery systems and collaborative processes at all levels. This is a unique venture and one that should have impact in all denominations and be of significant help in future training of ministers for small churches and the training of the laity as well. It obviously could have major impact on national programs, seminary education, and administrative structures. Breakdown figures from the various denominations on the numbers of churches of small size are very difficult to obtain.

To examine the overall figures, however, and to recognize that the average church for the Disciples of Christ is 271 members, for the United Church of Christ 297 members, for American Baptists 243, and for Southern Baptists 326, indicate that a preponderance of the churches must fall into the category of small. The Presbyterian Church, U.S., uses a classification of 250 as being small and has 70 percent of its churches in that category, with 44 percent under 100. It is obvious why this latter group has made the small church one of its six top priorities as a denomination.

The United Methodist Church has nearly one-fourth (9,464) of the total number of churches under 100 in membership.

The research and action by McCormick Seminary will have deep significance for all denominations.

Budgets

Many would name finances as being the central problem of small churches. But this assumption must be questioned. Budget is not the reason for growth or the lack of growth for service and ministry. To use budget problems as an excuse is simply to avoid reality. Budgets are critical but for different reasons than growth.

Many small churches are in financial difficulty because they are attempting to support a full-time ministry geared to the geographical concept of parish based on horse-and-buggy travel which provides too small a base. If there is a rethinking of the parish concept, at the very least gearing it to modern travel time, then the potential membership base for a church may be broadened. It would not be unhealthy if some churches were to merge, recognizing that they now live in a motor age with hard-surfaced roads. Budget problems, thus, are often the result of too small a parish based on antiquated concepts.

If a church fellowship or congregation is so set that it feels for internal reasons that it wants to cling to patterns of the past as far as the geographical parish is concerned, then perhaps a reexamination of the concept of a paid ministry is in order. Several denominations have developed forms of lay ministry and have provided for training for those lay ministries. Attention will be given later also to groupings of churches for the sharing of a paid ministry if this form must be maintained. But it is a matter of fact that many churches are having increasing difficulty in supporting a paid ministry. The inflationary cycle is too much. Some pulpits will always be vacant, and churches will be forced to link themselves with other churches in order to find a minister or to use a lay ministry or even to merge. Rather than drift into such a situation, however, thoughtful planning is needed by national and regional church officers as well as local church members.

A vital ministry does not come by drifting. It will come only by careful planning.

Careful thought must be given to the goals, objectives, and the mission of the church. Budget decisions are secondary to and must be based on program decisions. Too frequently the amount of budget is determined first; then program is decided by doing the traditional, using budget remainders, if any, for new innovative program. A number of small churches might find unexpected opportunities for service and spiritual growth if they were to determine first the most critical needs of the members and community and then base their budgets on meeting those needs in order of priority. If young people are left with little to do and delinquency is increasing, perhaps the church might set itself to this aspect of ministry for a specified period. In serving the youth and assisting them in wholesome growth, the church itself can find new life. If there are no child-serving agencies in the community, or if they are inadequate, perhaps this becomes a priority for program and then for budget. By so doing, the church finds a function in the life of the community.

But the point must be stressed again and again that budgets should not determine programs. Programs should shape budgets. A paid minister may not be the most needed emphasis at this point of life in the community. A church building may not be the most needed emphasis. Some churches have found a fulfillment of a mission without a minister or a building in a "house church." The traditional concept of program must not be allowed to snuff out the spiritual spark that is waiting to burst into flame.

"Where there is no vision, the people perish" (Proverbs 29:18, KJV).

There are two other aspects of budget concerns that should be mentioned briefly. Stewardship authorities in several denominations indicate that more than 65 percent of the small churches have no planned fund solicitation of members. Per capita giving is high in small churches, but it is not always on a systematic basis. Churches should challenge the people. Many are capable of giving far more, and if an adequate program concept were developed by responsible church officials, people would often give more. But where is the challenge when the church continues to be the same though it may be struggling? There is little incentive for increased giving when there is no increased vision or program or when the budget is a minimal budget for maintenance of life. In the experience of the author, there is potential for giving from members of the community outside the church if the church shows community concern. Systematic planning in both program and budgets must be accompanied by systematic opportunities for giving by the constituency, which includes more than the members of the church.

There is an irreducible minimum budget for all churches, whether they are large or small. If they attempt to maintain an adequate building for worship, education, and community gatherings, plus a paid ministry, a basic budget will be required regardless of size of membership. Denominations might well study what is considered to be an irreducible minimum for adequate programming in a small church. Many small churches that are now struggling need help to understand adequate programming. If reputable study by representatives from churches and denominations could produce this information and it could be disseminated to members of small churches, there would be invaluable assistance given in the rethinking of mission, parish concept, and size of the congregation. If there were a strategic ministry that needed to be maintained, then a basis for denominational subsidy would be at hand. On the other hand, if the church is not needed in the denominational and ecumenical strategy for the region, then church members would still have a rationale for decision. Owners and operators of a small-business enterprise are quite familiar with basic operating budgets and the concepts behind them. They would understand this logic in the church. There is a hidden value as well. Most denominations have not yet defined what they mean by basic program for the local church. If the thesis enunciated above is correct, that budget grows out of program and then by calling for a basic budget, basic program would first have to be established. Many denominations are following the concept of developing a variety of programs in order that a local church may pick and choose what it wants. Not all are expected to be used by all local churches at all times. There are different stages of development and growth among local churches, of course. This, however, often leads to confusion in the local church, for the philosophy is not understood. The plight of the small church would be relieved if the denomination would define what it considers to be basic for churches of various sizes and then put the rest of its programs in the realm of "electives." Budgets would thus be established that would be Christian in concept, for mission would come first, with budget being the tool to get the job done.

Leadership

Informed, trained, and willing leadership is obviously needed for such a movement. The author has been too long in denominational and interdenominational work to have retained any false illusions about the ease of accomplishment in securing leadership. There is realism, however, for there have been occasions when such leadership has been found. It will not be easy, for there is an anti-intellectualism in many small churches. This again is a vicious circle, for the very people of resource that are needed for new ideas are repelled by the unspoken or, perhaps, even spoken attitudes that may be communicated in some small churches. Many young people with their eager, questing spirits leave communities, both urban and town and country, in which there is little stimulus. The young people want a better future than is offered. As a result, a sterility and an inbreeding take place that lead to an emotional approach.

Some churches have recognized this peril and have sought for intellectual integrity while maintaining spiritual warmth.

Timber Lake, South Dakota, a village of six hundred, has a Community Baptist Church with an energetic, well-trained woman pastor, Jeanie K. Sherman. The church of 106 resident members serves an area of some 4,200 square miles. The church has been conscientious in its seeking to meet the needs of the people of the area. It has also been characterized by its preparation for the future in training young people and leaders of the church. It has taken in a literal fashion that there must be "an equipping of the saints."

There was need for a library in the area, and the church, with its pastor, became active in taking steps to see that this need was met. A tri-county library is now in existence, but with the vast expanse of distance this was thought to be inadequate, so a bookmobile also makes the rounds. Since 1945, more than fifty young people have been encouraged and assisted in various ways in their desire to go to college. Seven have completed doctoral programs. Miss Sherman, a seminary graduate, has been given an honorary doctorate in recognition of her outstanding ministry.

There has been a consistent program of keeping in touch with service personnel. A frequent comment is made that this kind of personal concern has led the young person to return to the area. The whole community has been helped, therefore, for it has not been as badly depleted in youth as other comparable areas have been.

Some would say that there is little need for any active program assisting youth who have been in difficulty with the law in a sparsely settled area, but delinquency patterns are not confined to the city. The Timber Lake church has not only released its pastor for service in camps and conferences dealing with delinquent and predelinquent youth, but has also made provision within the homes of members for assistance. Some couples have assisted young people who are in difficulty. In other instances, youngsters who are without homes have been made welcome into foster homes.

Many rural churches have read of interracial problems and have said that they do not need to be concerned since they are a homogeneous community. Once again, this parish, through its various contacts, its service personnel, and by other means has been concerned about racial and cultural problems. There are interracial couples who are members of the church. Four races are represented in the congregation.

The above is coupled with a strong evangelistic program and a sound fiscal approach as well. It has not been easy. The church received denominational support for a period of time but is now paying its own expenses and contributing generously to the benevolence program of its denomination.

An active program has not been enough, however, for it has been recognized that there is need within a Christian group to have a thorough grounding in Christian principles. There are organized Bible study groups on various weeknights in homes within the area. These may be widely scattered and are dependent in many instances upon leadership from the laity of the church. By this means, not only training but also fellowship is provided in this sparsely settled area. While the church is related to the American Baptist Churches in the U.S.A., it has within its congregation people coming from diverse denominational connections because of the concern and personal interest in the church for all of the people of the community.

Reference has already been made to "the family chapel" type or small church which for ethnic or other reasons has only people related by marriage or blood in it. Any outsider, including the minister, is viewed with complacency if not outright suspicion. This type of situation makes planning meetings or church business meetings unproductive. Decisions are often made, not at the formal meeting, but in other gatherings of "the clan." Reactions can be anticipated, too, because of the intimate knowledge the people have of each other, and machination can take place in advance to thwart any idea that may be "out of step." Enthusiasm and creativity are curbed before they have a chance to be aired. "Tiny gods" become the rulers in place of the Father of the universe.

Such an ingrown character alienates any newcomer who may be bold enough to attend. One may be made to feel personally welcome, but one's ideas are not encouraged. There is an air of testing and "wait and see" that inhibits the newcomer. Even in the smallest communities of our nation, there is a mobility rate among the younger and more aggressive persons that does not allow a church to have a "wait and see" attitude. Churches could be cited which have been thrust by economic and population change into places of opportunity for mission and growth. Sometimes the people of the church were not prepared for change and adopted a "testing" attitude. The newcomers soon bypassed the church that had been there for years. This "bypassing" takes place through joining a church of another denomination, the individual's withdrawal from the church completely, or the establishment of a new church for newcomers. Small churches cannot afford the luxury of being "choosy" or "censorious" even if this were permitted in the Christian ethic. Not only do they need the members, but far more important, they also need the leaven that comes with new and fresh attitudes and ideas. Too many small churches are small, but not because of lack of potential for growth. They are small because they have not accepted the mission which is "to go into all the world, beginning here at Jerusalem. . . ." It can be stated almost categorically that there are more people not actively identified with any church in a community than there are members.

Smallness can breed smallness when one studies genetics. While people may change some of their characteristics over a long period of years because of diet, better living conditions, and similar factors, it is also true that family characteristics are perpetuated. Small churches must take care that they do not produce small people. Each individual needs to participate in some measure in the world ministry of Christ's church.

There must be a conscious seeking for new, fresh ways of worship. If a pattern resists change and begins to become predominant, conscientious leaders will recognize the danger and deliberately seek to vary that pattern. People may resist the changing of a particular hymnal, but new hymns that are in the old hymnal can be taught. Bidding prayers can be used rather than pastoral prayers on occasion. God speaks in various ways. A small church does not have to be limited in worship patterns. People of another faith can be guests. People of the same denomination from another community can share. The local schoolhouse projector can perhaps be borrowed for a fine religious film. A set order of worship can be varied. The church is responsible for spiritual growth and must take care to use good tools that are available for that purpose. In that quest for spiritual growth, intellectual growth can be a part of the process.

Some nations of our world are concerned over the "brain drain." They are losing their scientific potential because they do not offer sufficient challenge in their own scientific circles. Thus, their scientists emigrate because of increased intellectual opportunity or increased financial reward elsewhere. Small churches can be victims of "brain drain," too, if they do not offer challenge and growth.

The Clergy

One of the chief leadership problems is that of the clergy. There is little encouragement for a trained, qualified person to be dedicated to a ministry in small churches. If there are family responsibilities, the salary level and living accommodations will often be inadequate for what is essential. Denominational staff and fellow clergy will often question the motivation for staying and constantly badger the pastor to consider moving to "more challenging positions." The people of the church being served will have been conditioned over the years to expect a short-term pastor and will either refuse strong cooperation because the next pastor would change things or else will refuse cooperation by the outright statement that the pastor won't stay long anyway. The apathy that has been bred into the small church demands a long-term pastorate to change attitudes and redirect the energies and program. But that same apathy is more likely to infect the pastor by creating restlessness, inclination to move, or else by bringing him into the rut.

Many in positions of influence regard the small church as a stepping-stone to a vital ministry rather than a vital ministry in itself. They either lure the pastor into other positions or negate the work of a capable person by lack of support. No church that is needed and that is still fulfilling a mission can rightfully be regarded as a "stepping-stone" to a larger pastorate. The attitudes of the denomination, the staff, the ministry, and the laity must be reversed. The small church, because of its inherent handicaps, needs a better qualified ministry than many larger churches. Greater creativity in programming plus adapability, flexibility, and a challenging faith are essential to move the church from the stationary position that it has all too often taken for granted.

Often the lay leadership of the small church will sense this and will turn to a different type of pastor, hoping that there will be some stability. They may not look deeply enough, however, at background and experience. Ministers of "irregular" backgrounds who may be from different denominations and who may have incomplete training often in substandard schools, may be sought. They are often responsive to this particular kind of call. They sometimes feel that if they can lead the church out of the denomination into "the true faith" they will have fulfilled a mission. The tragedy is that the previously mentioned anti-intellectualism, sometimes present in the small church, is responsive to a kind of theology that is biased and completely inadequate in its exclusive focus upon personal salvation. To some in the small church, education is suspect and means "liberalism," and anyone with education is viewed with distrust and suspicion. The small church needs more, not less, intellectual and spiritual stimulation. It also needs more contact and involvement with community needs, and it needs to become a part of the community fabric.

The emphasis on a one-sided theology that stresses "personal salvation" and neglects the servant aspects of the gospel contributes to the further isolation of the small church and its deteriorating condition. It becomes even less effective in evangelism. While denominations are all too aware of this coming of the "irregulars" into the small church, the mission boards and local denominational units do not feel that they can justify any great amount of money being placed in the support of qualified clergy in a static small church. In these days of "population explosion" much of the money for pastoral support is being reserved for another type of small church in communities with high potential for growth. Low-potential churches are left to their own devices and take the road of least resistance, accepting a person who may ask for less and who may share in the support through secular work. The laity of the church does not always have sufficient experience to recognize the beginning of a new pathway when it follows this road. Any attempt from the denomination to inform them is rejected because of the already existing gulf between the church and the denomination. As a matter of fact, often the local church may act on its own, if it is congregationally governed, and call a pastor before any denominational official is informed. Independence is a fetish still in areas of our nation where people have had to rely upon themselves for so much. Where people must live by their own skills and are not as conscious of dependence upon others, they are not likely to call upon outside resources for the church either.

If a trained minister does feel a call to this type of situation and accepts it with faith and hope, there may be disillusionment just before the critical time of change is showing itself. Discouragement is a common factor among ministers in small churches. There may be a sense of futility, for they have few tools adapted for their situation. The small church as an organization has been studied by several denominations of our country, but studies are incomplete and application of findings is lacking. The small church is recognized as a problem, but, in its individual weakness, it is unable to voice a loud enough cry to compel the denominations to give attention. The function, the mission, and the form of the small church are not fully understood in denominational and ecumenical planning circles. The lack of books and pamphlets in this area is but one indication. Card catalogs of major libraries list but a handful of materials that are available, and many of them are now thirty years old or more. Because solutions are not readily obtainable when discouragement comes, the minister is apt to find it easier to move than to remain and to attempt to solve the problems alone. Many years ago, Roy L. Smith said, "Many ministers move because the churches won't." But the author has visited with a number of lay people of small churches who have said, "If our minister had only stayed another year, it would have been different. We saw signs of change, but he didn't; and so he moved just as some of us were taking hope."

Ministers of small churches, if they were going to a foreign mission field, would expect to take several years to learn the language and the customs of the people in the far-off land. Many small churches are in "mission fields." The minister may need to prepare for a different orientation to plan programs, organize, and administer the work that needs to be done. A minister may be fooled by the outward appearance of the same language and the same general culture into believing that he or she has an understanding of the parish. The latter may be quite different because of years of conditioning and the static situation which has forced upon the people a kind of Rip Van Winkle state of sleeping while the world changes. They need to awaken, as did Rip Van Winkle, into the present world. A minister who will stay long enough to understand the situation and win the love and support of the people can lead them into a new day. Perhaps it can be summed up in the graphic phase heard recently about one man who was facing some changes in his career and had to decide whether he was to be "called up or called out."

Reference needs to be made, though fleetingly, to the paradox into which some denominations fall. They encourage small churches to use theological students as their ministers. While it may be helpful to the student to use the church as a learning situation, it does not always help the church. The church does not need a "beginner" to come to try out theories for three or four years while studying. It needs a seasoned person who is reasonably secure in the understanding of the gospel and who also understands its proclamation. The small church using the resource of students is further forced into a situation of viewing itself as less than a regular church, for it settles for a short-term person who is just learning. It must be added in all fairness that some students, with their freshness of approach and eagerness to be "in the ministry," more than compensate for their lack of maturity when compared with an older man who may "settle in." Quality and age are not always synonyms. Again, the laity of the local churches is all too aware of this dilemma and, when forced to choose, may deliberately choose a student because of the student's enthusiasm. But if students are to be used, the denomination owes some supervision so that the local church may have continuity in the predictable rotation of ministers that will be established.

One other solution to the clergy problem that is attempted is to use a trained minister for several charges or points. The Methodists, for example, have about the same ratio of ministers to churches as any other denomination, but their size makes the problem a more dramatic one. They have 39,262 churches and 24,268 charges. It is obvious that a number of ministers serve several churches as one charge. While the total membership may still be small, the travel time that is demanded of the minister who participates in several churches and their organizations, to say nothing of their communities, means a scattering of energies that make for superficial attention. One of the churches can become a preaching point with the minister being available for emergencies only. That church may settle into the routine of acceptance of this as the normal pattern and will neglect its witness, evangelism, and service ministries to the people who are surrounding the church but are not a part of it. Yoking fields can be a solution if careful planning is done for a balanced schedule at all points. The author has visited in some churches where services may be held only once every two or three weeks and in some extreme cases only monthly. This is hardly an adequate church, for it does not carry a full ministry on a systematic basis.

The lack of fulfillment for both the laity and the clergy under such circumstances is one of the tragedies of the twentieth-century church. Expectations have been raised in so many areas that a standard church of twenty years ago is substandard today. People are entitled to have the spiritual needs of their lives met. When they persevere even under the adverse circumstances listed previously, they need not only sympathy and understanding but also the earnest support of all denominations and ecumenical groups. The damage that is done to church members cries out to the sensitive observer for rectification. While the potential for physical growth may be limited in many such areas, these are still God's children, and spiritual growth is their right. The fruits of the ministry under such circumstances are likely to be insecurity, small minds, biased personalities, bickering, and frustrated spirits. These are hardly the fruits of the spirit mentioned in Ephesians.

In a static area in the vicinity of Broken Bow, Nebraska, two Evangelical United Brethren churches combined with six Methodist churches to form the Custer Methodist Charge Council.

This council (established in 1964) is an interesting and provocative concept of meeting a problem that exists in many areas of the nation. There are now six continuing churches in this charge with three ministers serving on the staff to minister to the total membership of 1,370. Of the six churches, one church has 848 members, and the six remaining churches range in size from 60 to 196 members, these falling within the range discussed in this book. The larger church could obviously have survived and moved ahead in its ministry alone, but it sensed a need and a challenge. A council was formed with three representatives from each church. The council developed budgets and programs, participated in the selection of staff, and coordinated planning in such a way that the needs of the people of the churches and the needs of the people of the communities were and now are being met in a better way than ever before. A major consideration in the formation of the council was the recognition of a shrinking population in this region of the country and a shortage of clergy to work in the churches. The council began its work, therefore, upon the basis of a minister for each four hundred persons and provided a secretary for the staff so that the ministers might be more occupied with the task of the ministry than of management. The sense of common sharing is worthy of the attention of all, for these six churches have taken literally the teaching of Jesus that they are responsible for one another, providing a way for all to have a ministry.

The Denominational Program

The usual denominational program is predicated upon a church of some four to five hundred members. Thus, when such a program is sent to a small church, the church becomes burdened by organization that is imposed from outside. The formation of the suggested committees and boards is impossible. Too few denominational pamphlets suggest that the program is optional or can be modified. Such programs by their very nature must be quite general to fit churches across the nation. They rarely take into consideration the individual character of the community, but rather depend upon local adaptation. The church needs help in penetrating its own community, rather than in the promotion of programs to assist those who are already members of the church, or even more remote, to promote some general program of the denomination, however worthwhile it may be. Obviously there must be a balance in these three emphases in programming: community, congregation, and denomination. The very nature of denominational programming from a national level makes the latter two the dominant emphases, for considerable time would have to be spent in each community to identify its own peculiar characteristics in order to develop a program.

W. B. Cate, in his book *Ecumenical Scandal on Main Street,*[1] points out that local cooperation between churches of different denominations is made far more difficult because of the vertical relationships of the local church with its denomination. The flood of denominational programs and literature supersedes any local interchurch relationships. This leads to an internalized use of the church's energy rather than to external relationships to the community and the other churches in the community.

An allusion has already been made to the fact that the small church is often passed over in denominational life, for its contribution is relatively meager. The amount of energy which would be required in the enlistment of small churches is disproportionate in relationship to the benefits and attendance derived, say some denominational officials. But the question must then be raised about the church's relationship to the denomination and the purpose of that relationship. It is not always the same. Sometimes the church does contribute to the denominational work. Sometimes the denomination must send financial, program, and leadership resources to the church. Sometimes the church and denomination join in ministry to the community. It is a partnership with both denomination and church sharing their respective talents and insights. Too often, however, the contribution of the small church seems so meager that the denomination does not promote the partnership.

Because not much seems to be expected, the small church feels neither the desire to respond nor the obligation. From whom little is expected, little will be received.

It is somewhat natural that strong lay leaders will be found in larger communities and often in the larger churches because of the modern sociological forces of our day. They become the pacesetters and opinion molders. It is inevitable, in the sweep of moving masses of

[1] W. B. Cate, *Ecumenical Scandal on Main Street* (New York: Association Press, 1965).

churches, that laggard churches will be given a minimum of attention. This sounds odd, for it would appear that the slow to move should be given more attention; but if the church in that category also has in it only a comparatively few members, the simple pressures of time will cause some to be neglected. The stronger churches that are likely to move "on schedule" will receive the required attention. In the event that there should be a surplus of time, or of leadership, either professional or volunteer, the laggards will be given more attention. It is to be expected that the greatest results will be sought for the amount of energy, time, and money to be spent. Small churches do not fit into a pattern based purely on efficiency.

The same line of logic applies to participation in stated meetings of the churches of the denomination on a regional or national basis. The strongest leadership will usually be sought for positions of responsibility. This is based upon two factors: the inherent worth of the individual, and the following which the leader is likely to attract. The person in a small church may be a person of inherent worth and of leadership capacity, but, because of the size of the church and the potential following, probably will not be selected if there is a choice between people of equal capacity but representing different size groups. Denominations periodically become sensitive to this process, for it is a violation of the Christian ethic. They will then select a person that is a representative of a small church for some specific event or perhaps for a board, and then, having satisfied the guilt feeling for a while, little more will be done.

If national or regional church bodies were to be established on a bicameral basis, perhaps representatives would come from organizations and from the membership. In some congregational bodies there is a legal provision permitting delegates in ratio to membership. But the perennial budgetary problem looms up at this point, for there is simply not enough surplus budget in a small local church to allow the "luxury" of being represented at the denominational gathering. They are doing all they can, they feel, in keeping the local church alive. There are devoted members who may have personal resources that permit them to participate. Such participation will be irregular and spotty in character and is hardly likely to provide sustained linkage between the denomination and the small church. On occasion, these people will be people with free time rather than people of ability. This only adds to the tragedy, for to outward appearances there is representation even though that representation may not be of the strong leadership of the local church. Some denominations are now adjusting to weekend meetings, recognizing that lay people often are prevented by their occupations from attendance at meetings during the week. This has proved beneficial in a number of instances, but still does not solve the deeper problems of budget and the feeling of being needed, which is essential if small churches are to participate.

The Building

Very rarely is there a small church that has a building that is adequate for its needs. We have previously talked of three general kinds of churches in the small church category, the town-and-country church, the inner-city church, and the suburban church. There are churches in each class which have good buildings. But, more frequently, the buildings are either old and outmoded in concept or have never been adequate.

Usually the town-and-country church is too small for rounded programming and often lacks good Christian education space as well as a place for community gatherings. The inner-city church is often too large, having been built for another era in which it may have been a strong church. Now there are rooms which are closed off and may not have been used for years. The congregation itself may be worshiping in a section of the auditorium or may have moved into the small chapel, which is more easily heated and maintained. The building of the inner-city churches has space for community program, therefore, and many of these inner-city churches could move to a fuller and more satisfying ministry if there could be staff and volunteers for a weekday program. There rarely is budget available for this except through denominational subsidy. Furthermore, this weekday program may bring in a new element in the neighborhood that may be of a different racial or national background. The members of the church resist this for fear that the weekday participants will come on Sunday and hence their church will change.

The churches are often in need of repair. Makeshift work may remedy the worst of damage, but scaling paint, crumbling bricks, broken windows, and sagging doors are hardly attractive to the passerby who is seeking for a vital religious experience. There may be a significant ministry inside, but the exterior gives no promise of this, and, in fact, gives a totally different picture. A nonresident minister and the lack of paid staff may be evidence of the assumption that it is obvious the church is there and if anyone wishes to come, he or she will inquire. Hardly an inviting appearance!

There are a few pamphlets and occasional chapters in some books on church architecture about one- and two-room churches. Some creative thinking has been done in how such small church buildings can be adapted, but the dissemination of that material has been too limited.

A limited building usually places the emphasis on the worship function of the church since a church's first thought is usually for worship. But a preaching service is usually a one-sided experience, even though there are congregational hymns, prayers, and responsive readings. It is certainly not a dialogue in which there is an exchange of thought and in which communication takes place that will lead to the development of common goals. The Christian education program is normally a smaller program as far as attendance is concerned. Yet this program is often the source of membership growth, for increasingly the Christian churches of today are dependent upon the children of member families for membership accessions. This source has accounted for much of the current growth in church membership rather than a true penetration of the unevangelized in the community.

If the small church is concerned about evangelism through Christian education and also in the education of its members to the meaning of being Christian, then a partially graded church school is a necessity. Even if the building permits it, gradation usually requires a minimum of twelve to fourteen teachers. This staff can handle a church school of up to one hundred members. However, the same number of teachers will be required for smaller church schools if there are to be graded classes. A church school of one hundred means a church membership of well over two hundred according to average experience. This is above the membership of the churches which are the subject of this book. A church of one hundred will have a church school of about forty on the national average. It cannot supply the dozen or more teachers that a graded program demands, and compromises will be made. Such compromises rarely bring the desired results, for compromise is almost always a lowering of standards. Little needs to be said about the ability of teachers, for under such circumstances even the finest of teachers with the best resources available would have difficulty. If the church is in the kind of community where study helps are not available and where the community mores are against the use of such helps anyway ("we should use only the Bible"), then the Christian education program will be little more than a form to be gone through. It may provide for some fellowship and some limited study but will provide too little of the serious study and growth that is needed for Christian maturity. It, too often, can turn into a sharing of prejudices and reinforcement of existing ideas.

People will tolerate inadequate buildings and the struggle for high standards in programming if they know that there is a goal in sight. This later combination of circumstances, almost exclusively, will occur in areas of new churches with growing population. Here young congregations sense that things will not always be this way. They are psychologically conditioned to growth and change. Because they are making plans, usually for the next unit of their church building, they are willing to work harder to maintain standards in the midst of unfavorable physical surroundings.

An Adequate Field

The problem of smallness may be a relative one depending in measure upon the geographical setting of the church. A small church in a small community does not have some of the handicaps that a small church in a large community may have. The people in a small community may be accustomed to a "make do" attitude. They are not as demanding in having everything of the best today. They may be dependent upon mail order or going long distances to a city to secure some items for living. Their patterns of living are such that they are not as impatient concerning inadequacies in physical facilities, nor are they as impatient of personal deficiencies, for they often must be more tolerant to live in the physical surroundings that they have.

A small church in a large city, however, labors under severe handicaps. The people have a wider range of choices. The membership may be scattered, with little fellowship during the week, and perhaps even little contact. Its task of evangelism is far more difficult, for in its weakness it gets lost in the hustle and bustle of the daily life that surrounds it. If by chance it is a small church on a business street, then the church is closed when people are there, and, when it is open, the streets are usually deserted. Its ways of witness must be carefully reexamined, for the very people to whom it may wish to minister may literally be unavailable at the time when the church is customarily prepared to receive them.

The problems which have been outlined in this chapter are the more dominant problems. There are others which may grow out of these. None of them are without solution, and none are so impossible of solution that there is no hope.

Solutions can be found if there is a merging of interest and concern by all levels of denominational and interdenominational life. There needs to be agreement upon a basic program. There needs to be an acceptance of the concept of "adequacy" in ministry, field, and program. The usual success standards are not the Christian standards. We are seeking rather for a wholesome ministry based upon offering the best for individuals so that there may be spiritual growth and maturity. The definition can be made clear if the word "adequate" is used in contrast to the word "inadequate." The use of these words would help local church members and denominational staff do constructive planning. There needs to be a ministry for all age groups, with good concepts of goals and objectives developed. Each church does not have to do everything. The nature of the community may be such that interdenominational planning will take place and various functions will be assumed by different churches, instead of each being a duplicate of the other. There must be attention to the concerns and needs of the community, for the church is the tool which God uses in fulfilling his mission in the world. The church is not the end in itself but is the means for ministry. An ingrown church cannot achieve the mission that Christ came upon earth to make manifest.

The church must move outward to the areas of human need in the social and political life of the community as well as the personal lives of the individuals of the community. When the church begins to serve all, then it will be on the way to a discharge of its mission. If it remains within its walls, simply maintaining its life and ministering to those who come, it might as well admit defeat now and close. It can then free its members for attendance and participation in other churches and in the life of the community.

So frequently it is difficult to know where to begin in church renewal and mission. The needs are many and obvious and surrounded by so many opportunities that it is easy to be frustrated in wanting to tackle everything.

There are two Presbyterian churches in upstate New York near the St. Lawrence River that are yoked but in reality share a common ministry as they work in their own fields: Chipman and Waddington.

As a part of a wider denominational program called "Doorstep to Missions" they entered into their own local interpretation with "Operation—Do One Thing." The flier that announced the beginning of the program said:

> *"Not*—to save the whole world at once!
> *But*—to join with others *to do one thing."*

From a range of options, the people examined some of the issues of their community in an intensive fashion. Following suggested questions that had come to the pastor on a continuing education tape cassette from Southwestern Baptist Theological School[2] and a lecture by Dr. William Pinson, they asked:

1. Which problem affects us the most?
2. Which problem hurts us the most?
3. Which problems are being met by others in the community?
4. Which problems are we best able to meet?
5. What is the spirit of God leading us to do?

They moved into examining seriously the problems of youth, the aging, the poverty stricken, the unchurched, and those in prisons and jails. This was not done on some theoretical world level but in practical significant ways right in their own communities.

[2]Dr. William M. Pinson, Jr., "Strategies for Meeting Human Need," Thesis Theological Cassettes, vol. 3, no. 8 (September, 1972).

Stephen V. Doughty, the pastor, records the obvious when he says that some entered in the task more wholeheartedly than others. Good things, however, did come about, and the process provided a stepping-stone to further experiences. Some of the more tangible and specific results were the beginning of a preschool experience for children about to enter school and counseling by qualified persons of others who were in jail. A part of that counseling program was also working with high school young people. Fifty young people took part in a "clean-up day" in both townships, partially because it was needed and partially to indicate that youth, too, are interested in civic welfare and community betterment. A shopping service for the elderly was developed along with a medicine delivery system. In addition some elderly were helped with tax problems and forms. Others were the recipients of a "bake a treat" program. There was also a calling program on residents as well as those in the community who were affiliated with any church.

All this was not bad for a beginning and for "doing one thing" in one's own community!

These two churches have also been involved for more than four years in a study program that had an innocent beginning but has multiplied into a program that may have permanent and lasting value in more than these communities. The Waddington church (in town) has about seventy members, and the Chipman church is in open country with approximately 140 members drawing on a farm population in a ten-mile radius. Several years ago the question was asked, "What are the moral issues in farming?" The immediate response was, "There aren't any." From that innocent beginning has come a manual of some eighty pages plus a study guide that is now being turned into a seminary syllabus and course to train ministers for service in rural areas. The document was developed by a study group with ten farmers and the pastor carrying the basic load of developing the many case histories in the document that relate to ethical and moral issues in farming. Such concerns considered are marginal farm operations, watering milk, high-pressure salesmanship of unneeded farm machinery, illegal certification of breeding stock, taking farmland out of production, collecting from the government and then using heavy fertilizer on the remaining fields to wind up producing as much if not more grain. These eminently practical problems led the groups into the significance of their own faith as they followed their daily pursuits. The question inevitably arose concerning the role of the church in all this with a searching of the Scriptures and the bringing alive of the relevance of the Bible to the farm families. The study document "Morality in American Agriculture" has a subtitle: "A few practical reflections for lay people and their ministers." In its introduction, it makes the point: "The most effective form of Christian involvement is not through statements but through actions of individual Christian members." One interesting research technique was used in the bringing of seminary students for a summer's work not in the pastoral function of the church but in working as hired hands in some form of agriculture, checking on the moral aspects of agriculture. The farmers recorded that they felt the need of someone who would have a perspective on their viewpoints. The bonus was in the counseling and personal witnessing carried out by the seminary students. Now the churches are interested in continuing this unusual ministry by the bringing of more seminary students and not merely in the summer.

The spill-over effect in developing materials that may be used in seminaries and in larger denominational circles is instructive to persons in small churches who sometimes are dismayed by their lack of impact. The value is in the idea rather than being exclusively in the setting from which it comes. Small churches can and do generate valid and vital ministries and ideas.

Chapter

3

WHAT DOES IT MEAN TO BE THE CHURCH?

In the day in which we are living, there is a flood of books on the theology of mission and the church. Many of them are being widely read and circulated. Lay groups are studying them, for the books are not only easily accessible, but also they are designed for such study and discussion.

But to discuss theology as principle or theology without application is to leave it in a vacuum. The local church needs to make its theology a living, vital faith that manifests itself in the ministry and service of the world. The world usually measures people by what they do and then by what they are. But the matter is not an either/or proposition. Both faith and works are needed, with the accent first on faith.

The small church has no different mission than any other church of the land, regardless of size. It may use different methods to achieve that mission, but the mission of proclamation, fellowship, ministry, and service is the same for all. When the church fully understands that the mission does not end with proclamation, that is a step toward the fulfillment of mission. The local congregation must consciously seek to understand the fullness of mission in the world church as its first responsibility. Once it understands, then it must determine its part in the scheme and the pattern of work. Women who make quilts are accustomed to fitting in the small blocks, sewing them into the right place in the pattern, and then using certain types of stitches to complete the pattern. They do not begin haphazardly because there is a design for the quilt, for the individual pieces, and for the stitches themselves. Until they know and understand the pattern, they cannot apply themselves to working on it. This may be a homely illustration, but the individual congregation must understand the world mission of the church, find its place within the pattern, and then begin the work of making the pattern come alive.

Many local churches view themsleves as being complete units with no relationship to any other local church. However, there are ties even in those denominations that are composed of local autonomous churches. To pretend to be independent in this day is to live by an illusion. Sociologically, it is impossible to be alone and self-sufficient. Theologically, it has never been possible to be alone. We are a part of God's world, related to all of God's children, and we carry responsibility for all, no matter how earnestly we may try to avoid that responsibility.

The local church has a second responsibility to bring to each individual member the recognition of relatedness to other Christians around the world and responsibility for sharing with them. The church must not only be inspiring to its members and bring individual growth as well as spiritual understanding, but it must also encourage members to be conscious of the mutual responsibility in the community and in the inter-community relations they may have. To educate a child and then not permit the child to use that education is foolish. A Christian is trained in the local church for service, not merely in the local church, but in the community, too. The community, in turn, is a part of a nation and a world. The church is worldwide in ministry. Any other understanding of the purpose of Christian training is a travesty on the Christian faith.

A third responsibility of the local church is to be corporately significant. When the individual member is trained and goes into service, the task is not finished. There are tasks which only groups of Christians can accomplish. These must be done together, corporately. The task may be an expression on an issue affecting the residents of the community. It may be participation as a group in the life of the denomination. It may be joining with other Christian churches in the expression of a common viewpoint. But training of the individual is culminated in the individual's witness where the person is and the total membership's witness in other areas of human living. The Christian faith is private in its origin and beginning, for it begins with one's relationship to God. It continues in one's relationship to another. The cross has this as its deepest significance: "For the Son of man also came not to be served but to serve, and to give his life as a ransom for many" (Mark 10:45).

The church has been most uneven in its response to world change. Some individual congregations have been quite eager to minister. Others have made it a part of their faith and practice to resist by "a *return* to God." Response depends, in part, upon how change is viewed and whether it is judged as "bad" or "good." Marketing patterns have changed. Medical practices have changed. School patterns have changed. Small churches need to see the change, recognize its significance, judge its value, and sense that it calls for a new expression of mission in this day. Because the church is a voluntary institution, it finds difficulty in developing the degree of unanimity that is essential for action. Other community organizations frequently have decisions made by a comparatively small group that is informed and concerned and can command. The church as a voluntary institution may have a more difficult job of education and commitment for mission and action than any other organization within the community, but it has no less responsibility.

We can never cease to give thanks that God did not and does not regard his ministry as fixed and unchangeable. The gift of his Son was an effort to bring to the world this understanding. God did not vanish from the world after that event but is still at work through the Christians of today. Christians may not be called "pilgrims" in the day in which we live, but they are still on a pilgrimage to all parts of the world to bring the gospel to those who have not heard it, or who, having heard it, have not accepted it. This task under God has continued into our day. There must be mobility in carrying the mission and flexibility in regard to the method that is used. The vast array of discoveries being made in the scientific world are staggering in their volume and import. More is being discovered of the order, rhythm, and significance of the creation. In that continuing exploration and discovery in the physical world, proof is offered that there is equal opportunity for exploration and discovery in the spiritual world as well. A church that confines itself to "services as usual" is not only shortchanging its membership and potential constituency, but it is also losing one of the greatest dimensions of the Christian faith, the opportunity to participate in the mission of the church in this day.

The Mission

Jesus said, "As the Father has sent me, even so I send you." Emil Brunner has said, "The church exists by mission as the fire does by burning."

One does not have to be very alert to recognize that the "children of darkness" are hard at work in our world. The rising crime rate, the greater addiction to drugs and alcohol, and the change in moral standards are all too common manifestations of a darkness that is sweeping over humankind. Corporate evils, such as war, prejudice, poverty, hunger, and nationalism, are pressing priorities for persons concerned for moral and spiritual values. Christians live under the mandate of chapter 25 of the Gospel of Matthew—remembering that as there is a ministry to others, it is a ministry to Christ. Christian people are often timid in their expression of concern. Some hesitate for fear that they may be counted with the radical fringe of Christian people who often alienate by their method of witness rather than evangelize. Because each wing is viewed as radical, too many Christians wind up in the middle, which is hardly the place for leadership. Other Christian people hesitate out of personal insecurity, not knowing whether they will stand alone, or if they do, whether they will be strong enough to carry the battle through. Someone has said with a great deal of wisdom that "battles are sometimes lost, not by defeat, but because Christian people get tired." Paul's words are much to the point, "Let us not grow weary in well-doing."

There are two agents in history. One is God and the other is his people. We may think it strange at first to say that God, who is omnipotent, as we sing in hymns, is also dependent. But he is dependent, dependent upon us as his agents today. Often, when people in positions of civil authority and responsibility look for help and support, they bypass the church. When queried as to the reason, they will say frankly that they did not know the people of the church would be concerned. One of the author's unusual experiences has been to confer with police juvenile courts and others concerned with youth. Frequently they express surprise and then elation at the offer of help that may be available from professional staff of the church. The comment has often been made that "we had never thought of the church, for in our experience we didn't know the church cared. You are the first church leader to come to see us."

There are many fine people in the community who are concerned about moral values. Some of those community people may not be people of the church. God has a striking way of being able to use even those who do not acknowledge him. The church people cannot turn their backs, nor can they refuse cooperation with such concern just because it is not from the church in its origin. Church people may be surprised at how concerned secular people can be. Secular people, in turn, may be helped to a Christian faith by such communication and assistance. A Christian must not only speak out, even though at first his voice may seem lonely, but also must speak with force and clarity, though others do not quickly join. As an individual, one may feel one's own humility and inability, but one still has a responsibility to speak and to make it known that the concern comes out of Christian conviction and concern. Many fine Christian lay persons serve ably and well on chambers of commerce, welfare boards, and in other significant areas. Often, however, they fail to make it known that this is a part of their Christian witness. They do not need to carry a signboard or be obnoxious in proclaiming their motivation, but there always needs to be a quiet word at some point as to the reason for such service. If the light remains hidden under the bushel, it will hardly give light to the world. Not only is there the vertical relationship to God, but also there is the horizontal relationship of person to person.

We need to remember that Genesis records that God created the world and humankind. It was many centuries later that the institutionalized forms of worship began to appear. The Christian church, as such, did not exist until humankind had already had a long history.

God's concern has always been for the world. The church is but an instrument of God to be used to accomplish that mission. The church is not God's objective. The world is the objective.

Every community has problems. There may not be an actual racial problem, for example, if the community is small and all are of one skin color. But there is still a responsibility to be a part of the larger Christian community and understand what other churches may be facing in racial justice. There needs to be a training of the church member who may some day move to another church and to an area that is interracial. Just because a problem does not exist in a community does not mean that it can be avoided or ignored. The lack of a problem may only prove the isolation and the segregation of the community and thus of the church. There is also a corporate responsibility in the church universal.

Even the smallest of all churches needs to keep constantly before itself the concerns that exist in the community. The concerns may lie within the school system, the form of government, the hidden place where illegal activity is taking place, or in some other area. Regardless of where it may be, the church, as the agent of God and the carrier of the mission, has a responsibility. The small church may not have the personnel to have a specific committee for such social concerns, but, in the planning of the church, the official board can regularly docket consideration of such concerns. Church school classes can be forums for the mobilizing of thought and, eventually, of action. Talk, however, is not enough. There must also be action.

We are living in a world becoming smaller and smaller in size. The cataclysmic impact of an energy crisis almost overnight is but one evidence of the unity of world needs. The United States a few years ago had a grain glut. Today the surplus is gone, and the world literally stands one growing season from starvation. Hunger is a daily reality in our nation and other nations. The growth of population and the decrease in arable land pose problems which affect the person who lives in the most remote hamlet. The extinction of animal species and the overfishing of the ocean are causing extreme concern. The Christian must become more sensitive, aware, and involved, beginning with his or her own personal style of living. To use resources of the earth without regard to the future is certainly not in keeping with Christian stewardship, nor is it being responsible as one thinks of one's neighbor or future generations. We do live in a global community.

Today there is more and more emphasis on community organization and development. Many of the small towns of our nation find themselves in serious difficulty because of economic changes. Some have accepted the change as being final and have resigned themselves to gradual decline. Others have become aggressive in enlisting new factories or new forms of income so that the community may live. Communities not faced with economic change may be faced with sociological change. The age level may have risen, and the community may have gradually become a retirement community. There are many changes and many problems engendered by rapid social change. There has been need for the training of leaders in the field of community organization and development. The principles are varied and many and cannot be treated at length here. They apply equally to large metropolitan areas and to rural farm areas. Christian people need to be aware of these developments to see and view the work of the county agent, the welfare worker, and others as being a part of the service to the community. Their work needs to be understood, supported, and supplemented by Christian people. The church is not a private group, though it may be legally incorporated. It was created for a purpose, and it has a mission. The church is not a building. It is the people of God at work in the world making real the witness in the name of Christ.

In a relatively small community of 11,000 in northern Texas there is a church that has increased its membership in thirty-three months by 89 percent, its property value by 125 percent, and its budget by 500 percent. With a membership of 170 at the close of 1973, questions arise about what happened in the life of the church that brought about this dramatic growth, for the community had changed very little since the time the church was established in 1952.

As is true in many such stories, a major factor has been the enthusiasm and training of the minister coupled with committed laity. In this instance, however, both the minister and the church in an unusual act of courage had come together in a ministry that could as easily have failed, for the minister is Korean in a community where no other Koreans and few, if any, Asians live. Peter Suk, a person of intense faith, has a dramatic story. He was being taken out to be shot as a prisoner in North Korea, partially because he would not recant his own Christian faith, when he escaped. With privation and struggle he came to the United States to study for the ministry.

When the congregation began to seek for a pastor and heard about Peter Suk, they were heavily influenced by their own dramatic vision of a different world that was being born. There had been a shocking happening in the community when a young, black football player died as a result of an accident in a high school game. A kind of mystical experience had come to some of the men in the congregation of this Christian church that made them feel they had to contribute in some way to a better interracial understanding. This church in Mt. Pleasant, Texas, began its recent chapter then with a vision and a call. Peter Suk, with his own intensity of faith and deep commitment, fitted into that evangelical passion. The church, however, has not been content to rest upon that kind of mystical beginning and experience. Mr. Suk, by his own admission, sometimes has difficulty with parts of the English language, although he uses a total of five languages. He and the congregation, however, have instituted a community ministry as well as a preaching ministry. The church is working on plans for a child-care center, a senior citizens' recreational center, and a badly needed community playground.

A combination of deep personal commitment, community vision, and service has brought a church of 50 members to a membership of 170 in a little less than three years.

Ministry to the Individual

The local church finds one of its greatest responsibilities, quite naturally, in ministry to the individual. This is so transparently true that too often it is not completely understood. People accept it as a fact, without recognizing the depth. There must be personal evangelism. But the conversion experience needs to be preserved at a high level with conservation of the idealism, the dedication, and the intent which led the person to make the initial commitment. Quite obviously, if this were a decision of some maturity, the first emotional flush would wear off. This is to be expected and should be accepted as such. The experience, however, should be renewed on occasion, for, as human beings, we function on the emotional level at a good many points in our lives. Christian education, morning worship, and other forms of the church life must have emotional warmth as well as intellectual growth. It cannot be one or the other, for each has a rightful place in the lives of all men. The degree may vary depending in measure on the individual, but both elements are still present.

The experience in the church should be broad enough and deep enough, therefore, through its variety and challenge, to remind the individual constantly of the need to grow and to offer the opportunity for it. Small churches, forced by a meager reserve of leadership and being turned inward as they so often are, find little of the range and breadth of contact that provides this growth for the individual. The ministry needs to be a satisfying one for persons. Many small churches do an effective work in satisfying short-range needs of individuals. They provide fellowship, social contact, the form of worship which may be worthwhile, and serve many of the priestly functions in a fine way. But, in satisfying the priestly role, they permit the individual to become comfortable in his or her religious experience. The prophetic function, far more difficult to fulfill in the small church, and even in some large churches, must be part of each individual's experience. The tragedy is that some churches and individuals have never experienced this outreach through the prophetic ministry and thus are completely unaware of what they are missing in their religious experience. Paul says in Corinthians that there are four dimensions to love—length, depth, breadth, and height. The small church can provide length of love in fellowship and continuity, though it is narrow in focus. It can also provide height, for it does lift one in worship to recognize God as Creator and Father. But in the dimensions of breadth and depth, it is severely limited. The very size of its groups and its limited contacts tends to make it narrow rather than broad in its expression of Christian love. In its leadership resources and range of teaching it may well be shallow, repetitious, and confined to a form and ritual. A church has a responsiblility to its individual members to provide them with such experiences, understanding, and challenge, so that the present limited image of the faith will be shattered. It then has a responsibility to help create a larger, fuller, and more demanding religious experience.

The small church must look carefully at the needs in individual lives. It will probably need competent denominational and interdenominational help to assess accurately the needs that exist. Resource persons for such assessment are available. Then when some form of listing of these needs is prepared for its official board, the church may recognize quite quickly that only a few of the needs are being met and some of those in only the most superficial of ways. As has been indicated before in another context, there is a confusion in some small churches, for they look at the schedule of activities and assume that needs are being met because people are being kept busy. The small church must not confuse program activity and spiritual growth as automatically being the same. Individual church members have reported that although they attend the Sunday worship, it does not satisfy them always in their own personal spiritual needs. One of the distressing things in modern life is the frequency of this comment. When professional staff members open up this theme and document its accuracy for church leaders, their first reaction is one of disbelief and rebellion. But then, after discussion, it is interesting how many of them begin to note that this could be said by each of them about his or her own personal life as well. There is a hunger in the world today for values other than material value. This may manifest itself in strange and wondrous ways sometimes, but it is there. The small church, because of its lack in the dimensions of love, those of breadth and depth, will have major difficulty in meeting the full spiritual needs of its members. It should carefully consider, therefore, because of limitations of leadership and budget, rotation of priorities and concerns. Perhaps on a three-year cycle, different aspects of needs and ministry should be highlighted so that as a youngster grows, for example, over the period of a decade, there will have been exposure to some of the breadth and depth of Christian faith and concern.

A further responsiblility of the small church to its members is to provide the freedom for individual members to be themselves. Because of the clannishness in the small church, it is sometimes true that the members expect those who may be new in the fellowship to assume the existing pattern. "We were here first" is the comment that is sometimes made. The new member may not seek to change the pattern, but each should have the freedom to be oneself as long as exercise of this freedom does not violate the freedom of others as well. God's kingdom has as one of its greatest strengths the varieties of individuals to be found within it. Each has a contribution to make, and, in the aggregate, each benefits from the experience of others. A pointless conformity becomes a sin against God, for it denies the right of the individual to be free in response to God. Christians must always have mutual respect, understanding, and recognition of each other's rights. The small church must be careful that it preserves this mutual feeling and that in its own internalized life it does not inadvertently deny freedom to its members.

In its program, in its preaching, and in its outreach, the small church must provide ways of ministry that will permit each individual to participate in that ministry. If its preaching program is restricted, if its religious activity is barren, and if its outreach is of little impact, then individuals will not have their spiritual needs met. The small church then ultimately denies the very concept which it is seeking to achieve, a full-dimension ministry to the individual and the community.

Goals and Values in the Small Church

It has by now become apparent in this chapter that goals must be examined carefully to be sure that they are comprehensive, practical, and fitting for a Christian group. They also need periodic evaluation and review to test their relevance. Goals are always predicated, however, upon values that are desired. When a church determines the values it wishes to perpetuate, goals will be established in this frame of reference.

In the community of Kalona, Iowa, which has a population of a little more than twelve hundred, there is a United Church composed of Disciples of Christ and Baptists. These two churches had existed in the community for some fifty years when within a few months each found itself without a pastor. Each had been having a semiretired person or a student leader, and each had found some limitations in growth and response, partially because of this factor. In their decision to unite, one of the most persuasive statements was, "More people working together in one program would be more efficient and effective than having a few people struggle in two programs."

When the churches united, they had a total of ninety-five resident members. Today they have eighteen different denominational backgrounds represented in the congregation. They have been listed in the *Yearbook of Christian Churches* as being one of the one hundred national top givers to the cause of missions on a per capita basis. They have had a goal to give as much for missions as they use in their own local budget. They have made steady progress toward this goal and have found new vision and life in their desire to be of world service. This church has been cited twice in recent years by the Iowa Christian Rural Institute for outstanding contributions "to better living in Iowa communities." There were several times when building problems, different worship patterns, and organizational structures threatened the work, but there was a larger vision of what could be done, so this small church today ably serves its membership, its community, and the world outreach of the church.

Sociologists remind us that approximately 70 percent of this nation now live in urban areas and a far larger group is being urbanized. It is not the purpose of this chapter to get into structure of the church but rather to look first at spiritual goals and values out of which structure grows, as did the church in Kalona, Iowa. The church's pattern of today was originally designed for a rural age, but even rural patterns have changed in recent decades. The very hour of the service was planned for the time when folk would have finished their farm chores. Today, especially in urban areas, people may have several days off, and the Sunday morning hour may fall precisely in the middle of a span of free time that many need to use to renew themselves. God created the sabbath for rest and renewal. Physical refreshment is needed which, in an urban age, does not necessarily mean visiting the neighbors on the next farm, but may rather be a hundred-mile trip for a weekend. With many factories operating around the clock and shift work having the emphasis that it does, a traditional hour of service does not meet the industrial work pattern. The church has seemingly put a value on a rather rigid hour of service on a particular day of the week. The value should be on ministry at whatever hour the church can reach the individual. Traditional women's programs are being radically affected by the significant increase of working women. It is not enough to say that the church is open and that those who wish to come, may. A higher spiritual value is demonstrated by seeking for the person with needs and ministering at the moment of need and at the time of receptivity. In several of the stories in the Gospels, Jesus emphasized that he came to minister to persons and not to fulfill the letter of the Law. It is even more imperative in an urban age that the church recognize its primary value in ministry and not in the preservation of an hour and form of worship.

The rethinking of the role of the pastor is a critical need. This becomes a basic theological question for many congregations. Studies of the use of a minister's time have been done. These studies reveal that a large portion of time is spent in administration and in caring for the routine of the church and its members. Yet the question must be raised: "Is this fulfilling the calling?" Does the church hire a pastor (putting it at its lowest level) to act as a priest to the present members of the church? In the vernacular of some today, is the pastor comparable to the professional golfer at the country club, for the use of the members when they want him? Or is there another function of training the members and preparing them for a ministry of outreach? The minister is a gifted and trained person dedicated to evangelism in the broadest definition of personal and social change. The world is to be redeemed, not merely individual persons within it. If the church resists (and many do) the pastor's calling upon those who are not church members and perhaps putting those individuals' needs before the needs of the church members, then where is the value? What is the goal? For whom does the ministry of the church exist? Only those who claim it? Those who do not claim it need it more if the Christian gospel is true, for they have not even set their feet as yet upon the

Christian way. These are not easy questions for many churches and particularly small churches to answer. If the minister is aggressive and concerned, there are many involvements in the community and the area on a denominational, interdenominational, and civic level. Some church members will question this, not yet having examined the purpose and mission of the church, and come to an adequate understanding for themselves. They will feel neglected, for they may view the pastor as their own private chaplain and not as the spiritual leader, the evangelist, and the enabler of the congregation, assisting the members to reach out.

Who is to be brought into the church—only those of like mind? Inbreeding within a family leads to weakness. States have passed laws against such, for families grow stronger by bringing in dissimilar characteristics. A church that is composed of one section of the community and that does not have a representation from all sections of community life is inbred. It can become weak. To evangelize only the respectable is hardly fulfilling the commandment of Christ. Many churches are small because they have let their human impulses, goals, and values dominate. They are not putting the values of the Christ first in ministry to the least and the lost.

If a church has put the preservation of its institutional life as its first goal, this is hardly the way of the cross. Jesus was at odds with organized religion because he was concerned for all of mankind. Emerson has said, "Things are in the saddle and ride mankind. . . ." Churches are often in this position. The building means so much that youth cannot use it for fear of damages. Oil costs so much that the building cannot be heated except on Sunday. The fellowship of the present group is so close that newcomers are not encouraged to come for they will mean a new element to which adjustment must be made. The institutional life becomes the primary value and the spiritual value is lost.

The church claims to be revolutionary. Christ was so branded in his death upon the cross. In the book of Acts it is recorded that there were those who had turned the world upside down—revolution! Yet, the fact is that if the modern church is revolutionary, it doesn't show very often. Only in very recent days has the church become revolutionary in its concern for racial and social integration. But the church has not become as militant or as revolutionary in other equally needy areas of life, such as economics. The crime rate rises. Moral standards are in question. Pornography is easily available. The rates of suicide and dope addiction climb. Hunger is increasing. Penal and welfare systems are breaking down. It is a little hard for Joe Doakes on Main Street to see where the church is really revolutionary when the building is open only a few hours a week. Through the rest of the week there is little identification of the members as church members with any of the ongoing life of the community.

The church, and particularly the small church, needs to examine the goals and values that it has, the goals and values that it should have, and the ones that it places first, as compared to the goals and values of the New Testament church. The raising of such questions should not threaten the life of the church. If it is so weak or insecure that it cannot be objective about the goals of its ministry, then it is truly in a sad state. Every individual and organization needs times of inventory and analysis in order to determine the directions to proceed and the resources that are available for the journey. But to set program without first knowing the spiritual needs and goals is emptiness, for the program will be of little value in that it may meet only the personal needs which have been expressed.

In the Community

When the question is raised about what it means to be the church, the role of the church in the community must be understood not only in its practical application but also in the theological suppositions.

Jesus said, "I came not to be ministered unto but to minister." In Galatians, it is written, "In carrying one another's burdens, we fulfill the law of Christ." Paul left security, friends, and home to go into distant places that others might hear the Good News. The pages of Christian history are filled with glorious and triumphant accounts of mission work in all parts of the world. Often, however, individual Christians regard mission as carrying the message to a remote place where people wear exotic clothing and have strange customs and a different language. Jesus never propagated that concept. He "set his face steadfastly" to go to Jerusalem. He drove the money changers from the temple. He talked with the woman at the well. He called the nearby fishermen to be his disciples. His ministry was in the "here and now."

The church needs to be strong enough and vital enough to be expected to participate when people of the community gather to discuss common concerns. It is good if individual members or the pastor are placed on such councils, but the church as a unit, too, must be known and counted. The reason for insistence upon this point is that individuals are usually recognized as individuals and not normally for the organizations to which they belong. Belonging to a group and representing a group are quite different. In a community, if the church can be vital and have a contribution to make so that organizations will deliberately seek for representation from the church, then a victorious ministry becomes possible. The church will also inevitably attract others into its circle when it is recognized as a group with concern, though this should not be the goal for such involvement. The theology which is Christian is that of service. The church must constantly be seeking for ways to say this to the community. The community may be so unaccustomed to such a role on the part of the church that it may take years of patient education and participation for community people to accept the church in this role. Civic leaders will often indicate that they do not consider the churches of the community when they are making decisions, for they are neither sure that the church cares nor that it has the knowledge to participate helpfully in such decision making. Yet, if a decision affects human welfare, the church is supposed to be present and making its stand known.

This procedure will mean that the church may have to prepare a core of leaders to become disciples in certain areas of life. These few will meet regularly to study and understand the issues before beginning to express themselves. An ill-informed, pietistic, emotional appeal will not do the job. This is the level of the infrequent approach of the church when it does get involved in an issue. Even the smallest of churches has the resources to form task forces of three or four persons to study issues and recommend positions and action. Such task forces could invite persons from the community to join them in finding ways of action. Such task forces bring understanding and breadth to more than the task-force members. The task forces are short-term study groups usually and, as such, can secure attendance and loyalty, for they are issue-centered and do not bind individuals to protracted commitments of time over months and years. The church representatives, however, should be as well informed and understanding as the best of the community people. Then their witness not only becomes effective but also will be sought. Study and preparation are needed in all areas of life. It is not easy to be in civic government, in administrative posts, and in other areas of public life. A church member must exercise care that witness is not nullified by lack of understanding or by ignorance of the facts. If there are issues that demand a Christian statement, then let it be done with good reason as well as good faith.

The task is not to produce people to fill the empty pews of the church. This would be nice. It is also essential if small churches are going to survive as institutions. However, once again we must return to the question of primary values and goals. What does it profit a church to fill its pews but to lose its ministry and service?

It will be easy to ignore the small church, whether it be an urban or a town-and-country church, if:

1. It is not clear on its purpose and mission;
2. It is not meaningful in the discharge of that mission;
3. It is not challenging in that mission;
4. It ignores either the personal or the public ministries that are in the gospel.

It is not necessary to enumerate the frustrations, the disappointments, and the tensions which are often in the small church, for they are too well known. They need not be accepted as permanent, but they need to be accepted as a part of the reality of living. When they are accepted in that fashion, then they will be handled and they will become less significant than at present.

There needs to be an emphasis on Christian call and the urgency of the gospel and its application in our day.

In the estimation of some Reformed Church of America officials, the Church of the Master in Warren, Michigan, is a vital, small church that is moving.

Located in suburban Detroit, the city of Warren tripled its population from 60,000 in 1960 to 180,000 in 1970. The Church of the

Master in its ten years of history has had 150 families on its membership rolls, with 80 families in current membership. Only six of the present families were charter members of the church a decade ago. Because of the nature of the community in which it exists, the mobility factor is a constant challenge, for the average family stays in Warren only 3.8 years before moving on.

The church has had to run fast to stay even during the decade. Yet it has succeeded in reaching its present membership in spite of the community turnover. How has it done this? Through being quite willing to fail, some of its members would say. The philosophy of the church when a new idea comes over the hill is: "Let's try it, and if it doesn't work, then we will try something else." The church has majored in small groups, not merely for the Christian education of the church constituency but for fellowship and recreation as well in baseball leagues and other activities. The church has sought to minister through a crisis ministry in the community through its own Open Food Pantry with food being available to those in financial difficulty. It has joined in a variety of youth activities, not only on Sunday but also throughout the week, designed to interest, involve, and train young people. New persons have been enlisted through the vital and varied programs that are offered. The church has actively participated in several lay evangelism programs and has been effective as one looks at the congregation that is interracial and intercultural.

Today at the beginning of the second decade the church stands at a plateau, for its records indicate that it has leveled off, at least for the present. It faces the problems of an outgrown building and fatigue from the financial and growth problems of the first decade.

Yet it is obvious in the church literature and in communications that the church is not content nor is it resting. It is proud of its heritage of the last decade and is so committed to ministry today that some outside the Church of the Master view it as performing a vital ministry in the community in which it serves.

Being the church means having courage enough to minister. The goals and values need to be determined and the priorities set so that the mission may be fulfilled.

Chapter

4

GROWING POINTS

Those who are familiar with horticulture understand the term "growing point." It is the tip of the plant which is the point of growth. If it is nipped off, plants respond by creating another growing point from a tendril a bit lower that moves into the position. If that new "growing point" in turn is nipped off, the plant will respond by trying once again.

Churches sometimes lock themselves into a pattern which assumes that if one area of ministry and growth is shut off there are no options left. There are, however, many options for moving toward a spiritual deepening and even toward physical growth in even static or declining communities. Alternative growing points are available in human life, too.

It would be nice if there were a formula or a recipe that could now be printed which would insure this for all churches. A recipe approach is impossible, however. In fact, the creative cook in the kitchen will vary the recipe according to the altitude, the available ingredients, and the desired taste, as well as other factors. So it is in the local church. What may work well in one church would not work well at all in a church that might be within twenty-five miles. Churches, too, have individual characteristics.

If the church is interested in moving off a plateau or from the decline in which it finds itself, there must first of all be some analysis as to the present spiritual state of the church. Contentment, apathy, resignation, defeat, despair—all are words that have different meanings and also represent different starting points in the life of a local church. Whatever the factor or whatever the label, it must be recognized, accepted, and handled. These problems cannot be smoothed away by the wave of a fairy's wand. They are hard realities. Yet patience and faith have proven on many occasions that these need not be insuperable difficulties. They can be overcome. The resolution of the people of the church is primary. If they are determined not only to keep the church alive but also to keep it alive in a state of vigorous health, ready for work, then a major part of the battle is won.

The local church is not left to its own devices in such a decision and acceptance of mission. The staff members of the denomination are prepared to be of support and assistance and can often provide valuable counsel to a church that is genuinely ready to go forward. From whatever source, there must be a catalytic agent injected into the process. It may be a lay person in the local church who is willing to undertake that role. It may be in a contractual relationship with denominational staff who will provide sustained, continuing guidance for a protracted period of time. It may be in the calling of a minister who is carefully selected, not for the traditional role which the church may have been following, but for the change in skills which the minister may represent. Inertia is a principle in physics that holds that a body that is at rest takes more energy to get moving again than it does to keep it moving once started. Churches which have stopped moving or which have gone into reverse will obviously consume more effort than a church that is moving forward.

The Planning Process

There must be understanding of the condition of the church. Its mood, state of health, or whatever word is appropriate, must be carefully analyzed so that the diagnosis is the correct one. This process may take some months, including personal interviews and questionnaires to determine the state of being of the individuals and thus of the corporate group. From such an analysis, goals and objectives will begin to emerge. Eventually a plan of action can be formulated. This planning process may sometimes seem laborious and unnecessarily protracted for some members of the congregation, but it cannot be neglected or short-circuited. Starting down the wrong track could be disastrous, for enthusiasms will be created that would be harder to revive if the movement ended in defeat.

Most families do planning for their living. Budgets, future expenditures, schooling for children, clothing needs, insurance, and the purchase of a home are but a few of the many things which involve thought on the part of the members of the family. Somehow or other a comparable process in the life of the church is not always understood to have the same value. The church is often one of the last organizations in the community to engage in a planning process. School boards, welfare organizations, highway departments, and town governments are all deeply aware and concerned that before specific steps are taken and persons are put to work that there be goals and objectives which are understood and accepted by the participants. The planning process does not have to be a highly sophisticated one, but it does need to take into account the expressed needs of the congregation, the community needs which the congregation may meet, the resources which can come from the church and denomination to meet those needs, and an outlining of the steps to get started. There needs to be periodic review and evaluation to see if the original goals are still meaningful and to determine if the steps that have been taken are the most worthwhile ones.

Most churches have some kind of trustee board. In a cynical fashion, it could be said this is because of money and because it is required by state law. But, when one moves beyond that particular board, it is also significant to note that in one denomination, only 20 percent of the small churches had a committee charged with the responsibility for evangelism, 3 percent had a committee for social action, and 5 percent had a committee for long-range planning. But decisions must be made concerning essential tasks for a vital ministry.

Each small church must become quite self-conscious for some months of self-study and decision. Until there is resolution and virtual unanimity on the part of the people of the church as to their purpose, the plight of the church will become only more difficult.

In Colorado there is a church which was established in 1889 but did not have a full-time pastor on a year-round basis until 1956. During the period from 1949 to 1956 there were fifteen different part-time pastors. It would seem from the church history that there was some problem with goals and purpose.

Obviously there is a story, and the story begins at the point of a church that was established partially for a summer ministry in a mountain resort area. In the minutes of the church, there is the painful notation that during 1939 and following that arrangements were made to hold one service a month during the winter for the small, local community, but finally even that was discontinued because there was "too small attendance."

The building has recently been expanded with a new, badly needed addition which is used at least in part as a community hall. The church moderator wrote in his annual report in 1973:

> Through the decades since its inception, the fortunes and the outlooks for the future of the Church in the Wildwood have varied. There were times when it appeared that the church might become just another monument beside the road, a forlorn reminder of days long past. For awhile it seemed there were simply not enough people in the community interested enough in the church to sustain it. As the original founders passed on, enthusiasm and interest waned, services were held infrequently, and the congregation was able to maintain its continued existence only through mission help from the Board for Homeland Ministries and the State Conference [of the United Church of Christ].
>
> However, it would not be entirely correct to say that within the last decade, our church has been experiencing a rebirth. True faith and vision never really ever die. Neither do they lie entirely dormant. Today, our church seems well on its way to become all of those things that the founding pioneers dreamed for it from the beginning. In mid-August of this year, we dedicated the new Fellowship Wing. On that happy occasion, friends and well-wishers converged from almost every point of the compass. Nearly all of our visitors were unanimous in their praises that the architecture of the new building so well harmonize with that of the old structure!

> Our church has the reputation of a warm and friendly congregation. Let us cherish the image—doing all that we can to further enhance it!

The letterhead of the church is fascinating, for it indicates something of the dilemma of the church as it seeks to identify itself and yet remain open to all who are in the area. It is "the Church in the Wildwood," "a congregation of the United Church of Christ," and "a Community Church." As the only Protestant church in the Ute Pass, Colorado, area, it customarily has two services each Sunday morning in the summer and even then at the second service has some difficulty in seating all the people. It has now become, in the words of the pastor, J. Paul Tatter, a "bedroom community" for Colorado Springs and thus has really moved beyond the category of a "small church," having 250 members officially on the books. Many of these, however, are nonresident, being in some instances summer residents, students, service personnel, and comparable mobile people.

As one reads the record of the church, including the Sunday bulletins, it becomes quite apparent that though it is in a mountain community, thus with the temptation to be withdrawn, in reality the church is sensitive to wider concerns. It has participated and shared in financial campaigns that often would have little appeal to such a community—one for black colleges, for example. In the notes about midweek gatherings, frequently the topic for study has been a social issue of pressing importance in today's world. Some of the Christian education courses on Sunday mornings have been topical in nature as well, dealing with problems of personal growth, social issues, and kindred matters, rather than the traditional Bible study sessions.

It has related its program to the world in which people live. In 1956 it made a difficult and pivotal decision that in retrospect was more critical than perhaps the members of the congregation had expected it to be. Until that time they had used vacationing ministers for supply work during the summer and men from the surrounding area who would come in on occasion throughout the winter. In 1956 in a real venture of faith they called their first full-time year-round minister. J. Paul Tatter, who is now there, is the second full-time minister the church has had. A full-time ministry has helped the church move. Undoubtedly other factors in the growth of the church have been in part the constant change which has been thrust upon the church by the resort community. It has been "opened up" by that process. Full-time resident ministers who have had vision have supplemented the original vision of the people. There has been a continuing emphasis upon the study of theology and mission and what it means. The church has found a purpose, has set some goals, and has conscientiously moved toward those goals.

Only when all churches set forth a program that has specific objectives, with time goals stated within it, will they cease their drifting. Too many small churches follow general programs that are designed for the mass of churches, never recognizing that in some measure all programs must be adapted in the light of the needs of the church, its people, and its community. Activity without purpose and schedule without goal become empty exercises, for there is no focus. The danger of a ship at sea with a broken rudder has provided the format for many stories. A church without a guiding principle and a destination is in equal danger that may be more acute though less dramatic. Such a release from a drifting existence will not come easily. Specialized denominational attention will be required, and perhaps staff specialists may have to be employed within specific areas. But these, too, will be ineffective and meaningless unless all people in the local church become sufficiently concerned to pledge their energies and their most creative thinking toward the retrieval of a definite course of action. There will have to be periodic review to make certain that the church is still on course toward the destination it has set for itself. By this means will come renewal and a vital ministry for the church, not based upon the size of membership but the quality of service which the church is seeking to give.

Quite obviously, if a church is beginning a quest for a vital ministry, it must first have some standards of judgment about essentials that are involved in that ministry. There are various types of surveys constantly being published which comment upon the attitudes of the people of the local church. The things which lay persons consider to be essential frequently vary substantially from the things which the pastor will hold as being essential. The church people themselves often have such a broad spectrum of "essentials" that it is obvious that they could never achieve them in any realistic period of time. Many churches need to narrow the focus of their ministry, deciding what three or four or possibly five things should be accomplished in the next three-year span. The very process of decision will stimulate interest, concern, and participation within the church body. In the development of the methods to achieve these goals, another one or two of the goals may prove impossible and fall by the wayside. This should be welcomed, for, if in a three-year period two things were done sufficiently well that progress could be marked, the church would have a sense of accomplishment. Many small churches are sometimes frustrated, for they literally do not know where to begin. A stream may be broad and quite shallow. If it is banked and forced to narrow its bed, then there is more power available because of concentration of the water. It is better to do a few things well than to undertake too much. Agreement upon primary goals is the beginning of power and achievement. Concentration upon those few goals for an extended period of time will bring accomplishment and in turn will permit the people in the following period to turn to other priorities.

If the church is in a rural area, the resources of the county offices can offer help. The welfare staff, the county agent, school officials, and others will have data about the area that will help persons understand what is happening to the area economically, in population trends, and in similar factors. Similar data is available in urban areas. Often the denomination will have staff members who can assist a church in gathering such information and providing an interpretation and application for the local church.

Though the literature is all too scant, the state university may have relevant information as may the denominational library.

All churches regardless of their physical setting could study carefully the standards adopted in the mid-sixties by the denominations belonging to the National Council of Churches with regard to the churching of town-and-country areas. While the specific application is for those churches, the criteria do have relevance for all churches, including urban. Size was put into relationship with other factors, for it was recognized that the measure of a congregation is in spiritual stature and opportunity for ministry and not in physical numbers alone. These standards indicate that a community needs to have at least a population of one thousand for each Protestant church. It further provides that a resident pastor, conducting weekly services, with a program for all ages in both Christian education and community outreach, is a logical expectation. Many small churches in the United States do not have breadth of program. Obviously the people of the church community are being shortchanged in their opportunity for spiritual development if the church provides any less. Some considerable rethinking of the geography of the parish may be forced upon a local congregation through the acceptance of such standards. But, again, the question must be asked concerning the purpose of the church: Whom is it to serve? Those who are already identified with the church or those in the community who have not yet responded to the gospel?

Shortly after these standards were developed, the urban crisis and the racial revolution hit the nation. The resources and energies of the denominations were then redirected. Developing attention to ministry in nonmetropolitan situations was dissipated. Now these standards need to be dusted off, for they were not tested and found wanting. They were never used because of the movements of history. The standards, reflectively analyzed a decade later, are still significant and valid. The needs are virtually the same, and the solutions appear as relevant today as when they were developed.

Types of Situations

Not all churches want to grow. Some churches in areas with potential and large population centers have deliberately selected a style of ministry that limits growth. They have concentrated upon a particular form of worship or a "target group" of members such as those interested in particular activities or some other specialized function. They have found a small membership to be an asset and tool to be used in reaching a specific goal. These churches, in their discipline and sense of mission, need support and encouragement as well.

On Pebble Hill, in Doylestown, Pennsylvania, there are two newly constructed barns, one bright yellow and one red. They are the home of the Pebble Hill Reformed Church that early in its history also affiliated with the United Presbyterian Church to avoid having a stereotyped image in the eyes of the community. It has been successful in avoiding that stereotype, for one is more apt to read about the church in the news pages, editorial columns, or in letters to the editor than on the church page. Not all notes in the news are complimentary, for the church has sometimes cultivated and sought controversy, as in the protests against the war in Vietnam. The controversy has not been for the sake of controversy but out of a deep conviction that where people are hurting the church should be involved and take a stand.

Unconventional in many ways, the Sunday morning gathering is no exception. It is billed as "Celebration of Worship Action." Each week's gathering is a carefully planned experience by a task force of four or five. The entire congregation participates in worship—not merely the leaders of worship. Several task forces may be working simultaneously planning for different Sundays that may be several weeks ahead. Each service has elements for the whole family and is highly informal, with persons seated on the floor or in chairs. The experiences may be many and varied in a single service with rock music, dancing, genuine fellowship with "hugging and kissing," and a sermon that is more apt to be an experience.

The people of the church work hard at understanding themselves and why they are there in the church. Though they have no church school as such, there is Christian education on a family basis with study and understanding of the role of parents in Christian nurture. Its current membership, including children, is 210 as compared to 187 two years ago. Its current budget is over $40,000, including some denominational subsidy.

Gordon Dragt, who is the pastor, would probably deny his singular role in the life of the church and perhaps rightly so, for the people in the church participate in the leadership, including worship, as much as does the pastor. Gordon, as he is known by his own preference, was there first in 1968 and worked some six months before the first service was held. Presumably the recruitment came out of a carefully conceived objective which is partially reflected in the statement of some of the literature, "not trying to imitate an established congregation, but doing a new thing." Mr. Dragt has extensive training and background which he is using effectively not only in Doylestown but also other places in lectures and in publication. He has skills in the renewal of the church, new forms of worship, and has systematically been involved in human-growth laboratories. He knows how to motivate people to do for themselves and would probably prefer the term "enabler" rather than "leader."

In ministering in this community in Bucks County, Pennsylvania, there is opportunity to appeal to a different group, for the county has art colonies and persons of leadership and intellectual capacity who are not afraid of innovation. The Pebble Hill Church in its printed materials and in its program has recognized people who all too often need ministry but are not always given it. It has a producing company for drama and concerts. It has a coffeehouse ministry. It has a preschool for four- and five-year-old children. It has accepted change and controversy as being a part of the Christian faith and is secure in its own theological and sociological basis for being. It conscientiously seeks to be "consistent in caring" and has deliberately limited the structure of the church with its traditional committees in order that people might be free to be actively involved in community groups and issues where leadership and participation are needed. At times it has been regarded by members of the community as a political unit, as an activist group, as persons who get into everything. The church as such has not resisted those labels but has accepted them as being a part of the Christian faith and commitment. It has accepted its ministry and its place in the community and is being faithful in its own unique call "not to imitate the established congregation." In a personal letter, Gordon Dragt closes with these words:

> Pebble Hill Church is a small church, and this is our strength! We try to build upon our strength. We can offer things to people other churches don't seem to be able to offer; therefore, we provide an essential ministry to the general Bux-Mont area. For us our size is not a disadvantage—it's an advantage!

Some churches are small because they have had limited vision and thus have not known how to develop an attractive program that will help them to grow.

Other churches have found themselves located by circumstance or economic and physical change in communities that have declined. Some churches have accepted that circumstance and have realized that those who remain need and deserve a ministry. They are to be commended for that continuation of ministry. Their definition of an adequate field under the National Council standards will be different because of the continuing necessity for ministry. To accept without thought such a situation, however, may mean a sacrifice of a potential ministry that would be significant elsewhere. There is no stigma in a church's relocating in order to serve more people if it has first examined its motivation. If the community which it is leaving is having its needs met and if the community to which it is going is not being adequately served, then a move is most definitely in order. It will be tragic, however, if a church leaves an area without ministry to move to a community where it will offer only a duplication of a church that is already there. To be merely a representative of a denomination that is not currently represented is a dubious basis for ministry.

An adequate field whether it is geographical or programmatic is mandatory for spiritual vigor. The adequacy of the field may be measured by the number of people to be served, the needs to be met, and the relevancy of the group seeking to serve. Not all factors are equal or the same, for the motivation for ministry is a factor, also.

Churches cannot live for the present only, for the Christian cause is God working in history. Churches must be conscious of the long stream of history and their responsibility for their part in it. Moral and spiritual vacuums will be filled just as nature fights to fill a physical vacuum. Amoral and even immoral forces have moved into inner-city areas when churches have moved out. The mission of the church is not to members, but to people in need. No church has a right to leave a spiritual vacuum. If it does move, it must also plan for the community that is left behind as well as for the one to which it is going. It must carry fiscal, moral, and leadership responsibility for many years after that move.

Some churches remain small because they reach a plateau and become "typed" in the eyes of the community. People outside the church think they know the church even though they may not. In one denomination it was found that new churches must reach one hundred members in the first eighteen months, and two hundred members in the next two years. If they fail to do so, they probably will require seven years to reach the two hundred mark. People are conditioned by success, though spiritual leaders may wish they weren't. The "image" that is presented is important. If the church seems moribund and listless, it will not be attractive to those who are outside its walls.

Some churches in urban areas have seen new apartment houses being erected and have thought that automatically they would reap the harvest of more people. They have blinded themselves to the fact that apartment-house dwellers are often people who deliberately isolate themselves and are most difficult to reach. In still other instances, the new residents in those apartments may represent another racial or cultural group which the church is not prepared to reach and perhaps does not even want to reach because of the drastic changes that might be required. The people of the church are often reluctant to face the facts of life, preferring in many instances to dwell in a land of myth and self-deception and thinking that the facts are either different or will change by wishful thinking.

One decision may be not to seek for a larger and more congenial community, but rather to seek for a larger means of service. A small church does not necessarily mean a weak church, nor does it mean an ineffective church. Some churches of fifty members ministering to special racial and cultural groups have more of the marks of a basic Christian community than other churches of 1,500 members that may have become social clubs. The criteria of service need to come from the Christian faith and be adapted to the environment being served. The church needs to examine carefully its biblical basis for mission and then find within that basis the task it is to perform. The solutions are not always in finance and membership alone but may well be in vision and call. The United Presbyterian Church, with more than one thousand churches of less than fifty members, has given considerable attention to this ministry and has challenged itself, its churches, and other denominations to develop a new strategy for ministry through the small churches.

The Presbyterian Church, U.S. (sometimes called the Southern Presbyterians), has adopted six national priorities of which concern for the small church is one. In the near future it is expected that among the six priorities the small church will move toward the top. It classifies churches of 250 as being small and has 70 percent of its congregations at 250 or under with 44 percent having less than 100.

What Are the Values of the Small Church?

The proximity of work and worship is an asset of some small churches that cannot be dismissed lightly or easily. When a person works in one community, lives in another, has friends in a third and fourth, and worships in a fifth, life becomes disjointed, and the individual finds great difficulty in participating with enthusiasm at any point. If the small church has around it an identifiable community with much of its membership within that community, it is indeed fortunate in its assets. The people of the church will find common concern in the same community problems. They will find a growing unity in the daily crossing of their paths and the informal contacts which will be theirs. The church whose members rarely see each other except in worship and whose members live in separate, unrelated communities will find greater difficulty in uniting the congregation in fellowship, service, and common concern. A small church in this latter situation needs to look carefully to determine if a basic reason for its smallness is that its members have little to bind them together in witnessing fellowship. The proximity of worship and work is an asset on which many small churches can build.

The personal relationships can be another asset, therefore, if the members do have continuing contacts with each other in a variety of situations. Worship is excellent, but it is not enough. Fellowship is essential, but it is not enough. Work is valuable, but it is not enough. These must all be present with service and witnessing if the church is truly to have a breadth of program and continuity of interest for the members of the church.

Some people have acknowledged quite frankly that they like to attend a large church in order to get lost, thus relieving themselves of any participation in the ongoing life of the church. They use the church for their own personal needs but have not really made a commitment to the Christian community and its concept of service. Such a situation obviously cannot exist in a small church, for strangers stand out and are immediately noted and become involved. For those who are concerned and dedicated to the small church, friendship ties are easily formed within the fellowship that carry over into other aspects of life. Most persons want to be active and feel a part of the group. The small church makes this far easier. Word concerning fellow members can be shared more readily and naturally as well. Organization is necessary in a large church to accomplish that which comes quite naturally and relatively easily in a small church. For those who want strong personal relationships, it is easier to establish these in the setting of the small church.

If a church is so situated that its members must make a special trip to get there and do not pass it in the normal routine of the day, then it must have other assets which will overcome this liability. If the church has no identifiable community and thus has had its channels for effective local service and evangelism cut off, then it will need other assets to overcome this liability. If, by chance, the church has neither community nor immediate, natural constituency, then the church may be in such a dire situation that it is virtually irremediable. It may be possible to move under such circumstances and find new life, but to remain in the present location with these two conditions will mean a slow death. Some modern highway systems have cut communities, for example, and have created this situation.

A small church has an asset that is most significant if it is located in an identifiable community, whether that community is a neighborhood of a city or a small village. A small church in a large, vague community will have trouble in securing attention and being recognized. However, a favorable physical location must be followed by an active program of concern.

Relevance of the small church to the community and to its members is thus a natural outgrowth if there is sensitivity and vision. The educational process will be less demanding because the observable need for witness will be more common to all. Many larger churches with scattered members and scattered interests are able to mobilize support and activity. But on a proportionate basis there are fewer participants and there is more preparation time that is needed before the task can be started.

A small church does have assets, but it is more quickly susceptible to the absence of these assets as well, for it has too small a reservoir of strength in members and finances to be able to withstand such conditions.

In 1900, the Christian population in the world was 34 percent of the total. In 1955, only 31 percent of the world was Christian. Research projections indicate that by the year 2000, Christians will be only 16 percent of the world population. The population explosion is so great that evangelism is not keeping pace. Christians have always been a minority, and the pages of history reveal that the greatest progress and mission efforts have come when people have recognized that being in the minority does require courage, for it is always an uphill struggle. There are more who do not care or who are opposed than who support. The risk of misunderstanding and misinterpretation is far greater. But there are advantages, too. The spirit and dedication of the committed person becomes more pronounced. There is more willingness to break out of the mold. There is a deeper feeling that there is more to be gained than lost because of the precarious status. Smallness, too often, is made the excuse for failure in the twentieth-century church. In the first century smallness was a mark of respect, for the first-century Christian felt the keener need to witness because he was in such a group and because he had a cause in which he believed.

There is potential in each community in which the church may be located, whether it be town and country, suburban, or inner city. The major Protestant groups in the nation have 20 percent of their members living in communities other than that in which their local church membership is located, sometimes even outside the state. These people need to be "rewon." On any given Sunday, two-thirds of the people in the United States are engaged in pursuits other than attendance at church services. In the military forces of the United States it is accepted as a working thesis that 3 to 5 percent of personnel have a deep religious commitment. Obviously there is a great potential for the small church, even in a small community. If the village has some three hundred people and has two churches of fifty members each, simple arithmetic would indicate that both churches could double in size and still leave one-third of the community with no church relationship. The wistfulness for larger fields of service often blinds those who are there to the potential that is not being tapped. The old story of familiarity has led some churches into the trap of the acceptance of the status quo.

One denominational staff person was a guest in the pulpit of a small church one Sunday. He was requested to give an invitation to join the church at the close of the service. When he went into the pulpit and saw the size of the congregation, he was startled at the request but did as he had been asked. After the service, he questioned the reason for the invitation and pressed the church officer a bit by asking, "Were you prepared to handle the new person if one had come forward?" The answer came, "We didn't really expect anything to happen, but it was so nice to hear the invitation given." No work had been done in the community. No calls had been made. No new persons were expected. It was a pleasant bit of nostalgia for the church. There must be expectation and a willingness to work toward the fulfillment of that expectation if anything is going to happen.

Ecumenical Strategy

As has already been indicated, there are communities which cannot be neglected or deserted. They need a ministry. The church universal has no recourse but to recognize that responsibility. The burden is not, however, upon any single, local church exclusively. The denomination of which the local church is a part also has responsibility as do the denominations together. Individual denominations need to have carefully determined plans of church placement correlated with leadership needs. In turn, as denominations look at the areas of strength and weakness which they have, in company with opportunities for the establishment of new churches, there needs to be ecumenical cooperation and planning. For churches to rush to a new community with high potential and compete with each other is hardly good stewardship and certainly is not Christian. Each denomination should accept its proportionate responsibility for communities of high-potential areas as well as for those that are not.

If ecumenical groups would plan on a state or even a multi-state basis, particularly in sparsely settled areas, then there would be opportunity for people in all communities to have a well-rounded ministry available to them. Some church authorities are insisting that while it is true that some communities are overchurched, they may still be underprogrammed. In some instances, such planning cannot always take place through a council of churches, for some key churches would not cooperate in such a venture. A temporary planning committee may need to be created, perhaps under the auspices of a short-term special group to bring about the greatest possible participation. But it is essential that planning takes place and that every effort be made to involve the greatest number of denominations possible. The goal is so challenging that group loyalties cannot be allowed to interfere. Concerned lay persons need to make this view quite clear and not let the principle be lost. No individual denominational loyalty should be allowed to stand in the way of maximum ministry to all the people of the region.

In 1934 the Federated Church of Rochester, Vermont, was formed by the bringing together of the United Methodists, the United Church of Christ, and the Universalist groups in the community. The church today is officially affiliated with the first two groups.

It works at serving the community in which it is located and among other innovative features has Bible study on Tuesday with classes following each other rather than being simultaneous. One class is for ecumenical Bible study and the next is Bible study for beginners.

In contrast to some small churches this church has kept four boards in existence, but they have evidently been a part of the strength of the church as they have operated. The trustees, the Christian education, missions, and the diaconate boards all meet simultaneously. Listen to the pastor, Alan B. Bond, as he talks about the church.[1]

1. Geography plays a major factor, Rochester is isolated in a narrow valley. Therefore its institutions are stronger than those of its counterparts in the "outside" world. Rochester has a good sense of community, in part as a result of the work of the church, and in part contributing to the strength of the church.
2. A good sense of participation by at least some of its membership.
   a. Our by-laws which call for four governing Boards are taken seriously. Each Board meets for an All Committee Night once a month. The pastor cannot simultaneously attend all meetings and so the Board members have to take initiative on their own. . . .
   b. Our worship service includes a time we call Moments of Thanksgiv-

[1] Quoted from letter of Alan B. Bond, January 29, 1974.

ing. The pastor suggests a subject, usually keyed to the sermon and worship topic, and the congregation responds with ideas the subject evokes. They get the first Word before the sermon is preached, and frequently cover the subject very well.

    c. Arts and Crafts shows, flower shows, musical programs and other events where people can share their talents with the community. Creative people make a strong church.

3. An ecumenical Bible study, a Bible for Beginners group and Prayer Fellowship each contribute to the theological understanding of the people. . . .

4. The preaching is Christocentric, with emphasis on both the fact of the living reality of His Holy Spirit and the necessity to be socially responsible. . . . A member of the Board of Mission uses that time to explain how our mission monies are spent or might be spent.

One of the most frightening questions for a small church is: How does a church serve in a community that has lost its purpose? The economic base may have vanished and the reason for the community's existence gone with it. Industry has gone. The mine has closed. A new highway has severed the urban neighborhood. People are left, however, often with bewilderment and frustration. Regardless of the reason, the situation of such a spiritless community presents a greater need for ministry on the part of the church. Such a situation makes it obvious that hope, which is fundamental in the Christian faith, must be offered to the community with even greater faithfulness. The role of a "change agent" can be explicated here with some indications of help. Such a person recognizes the needs and by persuasion, concern, study, and enlistment of others who are ready for leadership begins to move out. Discouragement is a part of the pattern, and overnight success will not come. But a lay person with a genuine feeling for his fellow citizens, especially when he has a Christian motivation, can do much. By his optimism, work, and ideas he inspires others, and they, in turn, become a part of the process. The history of our nation is filled with the stories of men who have seen needs and have labored and persuaded their neighbors until the dreams became realities. The need may have been for a medical clinic, a hospital, a school, a library, a civic improvement, industry, or some other beneficial development. It has started with one person who has been concerned enough to begin. Denominations and ecumenical structures have a responsibility to provide or train such a change agent.

Formal structures within the community are often the most resistant to change and development. The informal ways of friendship, casual conversation, two persons enlisting the third, are the beginning points. Only after the "ground swell" becomes apparent do the official and formal structures become involved.

The Rebirth

Persons of conviction have never been threatened by being in the minority. The Wright brothers, Thomas Edison, Clara Barton, Abraham Lincoln, and Albert Schweitzer are but a few names that can be summoned rather easily to mind. An idea whose time is ripe and a person who is convinced of the need combine to present a chance for dignity and status to be regained. A man on "skid row" is usually a man who doubts himself. A church which doubts itself and its ministry may be on a different but equally disastrous "skid row." So much of a person and the ability to achieve come out of one's own inner security and feeling of responsibility. If there is support from family, from work, and from one's own sense of direction and conviction, the individual will persevere in spite of tremendous obstacles. A church, too, needs to have a sense of security, of responsibility, of being needed, and of having support as it goes forth to discharge its mission. Small churches need to be told by the denomination that they, too, are a valuable and integral part of the total pattern. Too often larger churches receive the awards and recognition.

In Mexico, Japan, Zaire, and other areas of the world, where Protestants are in a tiny minority of perhaps 1 to 5 percent, the feeling of futility does not exist. Here the people sense a mission. They feel that they have a contribution to make. They have an awareness of the difference that has been made in their individual lives. They are eager to have their fellows have that same difference in them. Being small in number does not bother them, for they have never been large. Thus they do not feel the siren call of size, emptied of function and meaning. While the United States has been the "sending nation" for

Christian missionaries, it is apparent that we may need missionaries who will come to tell us how to live when we are in the minority. Christian people in other lands are accustomed to being small. They are not dismayed nor frightened nor discouraged. Nor do we have to be.

Training Problems

The implication of much of the foregoing is that there needs to be considerable retraining for the mission of today. Some would view the church as a kind of safe-deposit box. One puts in one's life and then gets it back at the end, about the same, with little change or development but secure. This is a static view of the Christian faith. Christ calls individuals to invest their lives, even with risk. Jesus told the parable of the talents. The substance, when it is returned, may be infinitely different from the original investment, for it will have been enhanced and augmented during the period of its use. Lives are for use, as trite as that may seem.

But if lives are to be used effectively in our rapidly changing world, then considerable attention must be given to training of the laity and of the clergy.

For the clergy this will not be a particularly new theme, for increasing attention has been given in recent years to the refinement of theological education and to the period beyond that, to which the term "continuing education" is usually applied. Some of this training is directed toward pastoral skills and renewed theological training. It is too easy for a minister to lose touch with some of the effervescence of theological study of today. While there may be serious study and reading, there also needs to be the interchange of thought that takes place in the classroom and with fellow students. This needs to be sustained over a period of time so that, increasingly, periods of two weeks to three months are being established as times for opportunity for renewal. One observer has commented that too frequently pulpit committees seek for a man twenty-five years of age, but they want him to have forty years of experience. This, of course, is impossible, but if churches are that concerned about experience, then there should be provision for the minister to receive renewal and refreshment during the ministry. A sabbatical is not a fringe benefit for the minister. If it is the kind of renewal that it should be, and which is being offered rather universally these days, it will be a fringe benefit for the church as well. In fact, it is a necessity for the church and minister alike. The increased competency of the minister with personal refreshment will be of direct benefit to the church and its people.

There is another kind of "continuing education" which also needs to be considered that is not focused upon the minister as a person, but upon the needs of the field. There are specialized schools for town-and-country pastors, for inner-city ministers, for administrators, for church musicians, and for those in Christian education, all of which have value. They are directed toward the church, its community setting, and its program. These, too, may be of benefit to the minister or the lay person, but they are of greatest benefit to the congregation. A minister of a small church particularly will benefit from such experience, for there will be kinship with persons in similar types of churches. The feeling of loneliness which all too often saps the spiritual vigor of the pastor will be dispelled in part by such associations. The small church may feel this is too costly for a limited budget. Actually, not participating may be more costly over several years, for the minister can be encouraged to have a longer pastorate through such experiences, thus avoiding moving costs. The church will profit from the renewed vigor and refreshment of the pastor as a result of such experiences. There may be individuals in the congregation who would provide support if the church budget could not provide it. The denomination, too, may have resources, for many denominations offer scholarships that are virtually complete, if the local church will make its own arrangements for pulpit supply. The latter should not be difficult with lay persons in the congregation who, even if they do not feel they could give a sermon, might lead in worship and share in a brief testimony. Oren Baker, who has had a long and distinguished career in theological education, has said, "Seminary is an orientation to a task, and not an education." The orientation needs to be continued and renewed periodically throughout a person's ministry.

What has been said of the minister of the church is equally true of the laity. A Christian education conference, for example, focused upon the small church, would have inestimable value for a dedicated teacher who has been struggling. The opportunity to study, to visit with others from similar types of churches, and to secure guidance from educational specialists would give new incentive for the teaching task.

However, education for laity needs to reach much deeper, as valuable as the above example is. At any given time there are some 1,200 United Presbyterian churches without a pastor. There are some 800 American Baptist churches without a pastor. Other denominations have proportionate numbers. Many of these churches will not be able to secure a pastor, for they are too small. Their continuance lies basically with the lay person.

A church, when it calls a pastor, needs to examine carefully the reason for such a call. If it expects the person to preach, call, and counsel, then it should be equally clear in indicating that the other details of the church life will be handled by competent laity who have received specialized training. The church may wish to inform the minister that there will be a brief school for church officers in which they explore together the aims and goals of the church. These will need to be reviewed periodically for newly elected persons. But the methodology of implementation is no longer the responsibility of the minister alone. Many churches call a pastor who then is expected to become the church business manager—doing the banking, turning the mimeograph, doing the essential letters, and performing other managerial functions. The minister may actually have little time left for the pastoral function. The laity is not only capable of doing these administrative tasks, but also would respond to the sense of participation which would be provided.

Training should be offered for churchmanship. Besides summer conferences which are of help, there are often community or county schools. Many of these have been focused upon specific studies of the community. The relationship of the church with a detailed analysis of the role of the laity follows easily. All too frequently a pastor is not freed for what the church considers to be the primary responsibility of pastoral work and evangelism.

This is not to imply that these pastoral functions belong solely to the minister. There are many instances in which lay persons can be as effective as a pastor in certain types of pastoral situations. A trained counselor can assist the church in this function. A pastor may give immediate spiritual help at the time of death. However, a bereaved widow may be helped even more effectively in her adjustment by another woman who has gone through that experience with maturity and discernment. There are other similar instances in which the laity may share fully in the ministry of the church. The pastor of the church should not be threatened and, in fact, should welcome such fellowship and concern. The entire Christian community will be stronger for such a group ministry. The pastor will be freed for other tasks.

The pulpit responsibility is primarily that of the pastor of the church, but increasingly this is seen, too, as an opportunity for competent, trained lay persons. In the smaller churches it may be a necessity in the event of a church being without a pastor or if there is a yoked field with difficult travel and schedules. In some ways it is a tragedy that custom dictates a traditional preaching service when there are so many ways of effective worship that are offered and when there are so many books of worship which could be used by lay persons. If, however, the use of the sermon on Sunday must be maintained, then the pastor can make periodic use of church members in this capacity, but first insisting that they be trained not only in the mechanics, but also in the philosophy behind worship. The denominations have a responsibility as well. There are many lay persons who are gifted speakers, some even more so than the pastor. They can be of great assistance to the church and to themselves in their own development if they will consent to periodic responsibility. In Europe the Lay Academies arose out of the shortage of clergy brought on by the crisis of World War II. While these academies are not for training in the sense in which we are using it here, they were for dialogue and personal growth. In the United States today we may lack the crisis and drama of a world war, but we have an emergency when there are thousands of churches without pastors which, because of size, will not be able to maintain pastors. The sense of urgency says that more must be done at both the denominational and ecumenical level to provide training for laity in the meaning of the church.

Perhaps in this exploration and training it will begin to be understood that an extended teaching and learning session may prove to be as satisfactory and meaningful as the traditional church worship and preaching. Many have had the experience of having been in a classroom session that was so stimulating that the church worship and its sermon were anticlimactic. Small churches may not need both types of services for the personal fulfillment of the members, but such moves cannot be done haphazardly. They are too important to be left to chance—there must be training.

Alternative Structures

It would be most helpful in the Protestant strategy in the United States if there could be more consideration given to what is done in the Netherlands, where buildings and cost of upkeep are shared by various groups. "Pride of ownership" is too costly.

If a ministry is strategically important, and a congregation is willing to undertake a vital ministry, denominational subsidy may be essential. In most denominations this subsidy is a vanishing practice, for simply to keep a church alive is hardly consistent with the Christian ethic. It must fulfill a purpose and a mission. A church which is essential for denominational strategy in a region, or which may serve as a community church in a particular town, is valid. But to have four struggling Protestant churches in a community of one thousand will hardly enlist community support for any of the churches. Denominational subsidy will be more likely to be considered where a church is being creative in its approach to the ministry in its community. If the church on its own initiative moves out of the pattern that has inhibited it, then obviously other groups will be more receptive to approaches for support both in finance and program.

There are ways to move toward a vital ministry without denominational subsidy. In some instances, denominational subsidy may even be a limiting factor, for the church and its people become dependent upon it. In the experience of the author there is the vivid illustration of a church receiving a very nominal amount of support for almost two decades. That support was withdrawn. In the following eight months there were accessions to the church where there had been none for several years. The giving of the members doubled, and the attendance increased by 50 percent. The people were forced to rely upon their own abilities, and they responded.

If the individual congregation honestly cannot have a ministry on its own, there is no shame or degradation in that. There are open-country situations, inner-city ministries, and areas of sparse population where alternatives must be examined.

"Yoking" is one such option. It usually means that two or more churches call the same person to be pastor of each congregation. In some notable instances this has worked well. True, there are administrative difficulties in such an arrangement. Usually "yoking" is of churches of the same denomination; thus there is a common system, but often yoked churches maintain their own individual congregational organizations. They may do little common planning or sharing and have only the single tie of a shared minister. The minister is under considerable pressure in trying to divide time equitably, particularly when his or her residence may be in a community that is fifteen or more miles from the other communities where there are churches which are being served. The organizational demands of the various boards and committees become too complex and time-consuming. If the yoking is done by the churches simply in the calling of a pastor and there is no communication between the churches until the pastor resigns, this is hardly more than a stopgap measure. Yoking should lead to some gathering of strength with each field contributing to the other through joint board meetings, joint planning, and possibly sharing of the budget for some items, such as car allowance and housing for the pastor, youth activities, and planning for mission in the community and through the denomination.

Another option is in a larger parish which is composed of two or more churches, not necessarily of the same denomination. There is common planning and usually one budget though there may be several preaching points and church buildings. The administrative structure is simplified so that there is one set of church boards for the management and administration of the church. Because of the common process of planning and budgeting and increased responsibility and opportunity for ministry, often the church is able to secure and hold a better qualified and more experienced minister.

A federated church is usually a church in a single community with several denominational affiliations. Federation can be helpful in securing a more qualified minister. Too often, however, the federation is for financial reasons and building maintenance rather than uniting for mission. It has the obvious advantage of providing for a unified approach to the community. There is a peril in that it is possible for the church to become so enmeshed in various denominational functions of the several to which it may belong that it has no energy or effort left for anything else. There are problems of mission budgets, denominational literature, and meetings to attend. Many such federations exist and work well across the nation. There are strengths and values in such an option. If the community would be receptive and thoroughly study the proposal before a decision, it might be better to link the church to one denomination so that the energies might be preserved for a community ministry. If that is done it should be quite clear and the principle should be maintained that it is a community church, conducted by one denomination. That denomination should accept the responsibility in such a way that persons coming from other denominational backgrounds would feel welcome in the community church and so that they would not be led into the temptation of starting a new church, thus regressing to the pattern that had been dropped. The word "cooperation" is an easy one to utter, but when a church accepts responsibility for a community and does it in the name of one denomination, there needs to be periodic reexamination of the word "cooperation." To be certain that the principle is not lost, conferences could be held periodically with all state denominational leaders so that they would not be tempted to start new work in the community.

Another developing option that has considerable appeal is in the bi-vocational ministry. The World Council of Churches has renewed its studies on the significance of a "tentmaker ministry." The current theological trends make many seminary students impatient with the traditional forms of church life. The "worker priest" movement has captured the imagination of many entering the ministry. Variations of this have resulted so that some smaller churches through diligent searching would be able to find a well-qualified person who would enter into the life of the church as pastor but would find a greater fulfillment for ministry in being permitted to find partial support in a secular pursuit as well. While there might be fewer hours given to the institutional life of the church, if the secular occupation is more than simply a device to earn money, it can add strength to the ministry. Some ministers supplement income by driving buses and working part-time at odd hours in stores. This is not the concept which is being enunciated. Rather, it is a definite feeling of call on the part of the minister that being a part of the community and working as do members of the church assists all as Christians. There are trained seminary graduates today who have a strong feeling that they are a part of the laity, even as the laity is a part of the ministry. One of the apparent values in such a concept is the heightened role of the laity as it shares in the pastoral function.

An Expanding Evangelism

When one considers options for ministry, there must be a return again to the concern for evangelism. Some churches hold a narrow concept of evangelism, which sometimes manifests itself purely in terms of "special meetings," "revivals," and the like. But evangelism must be a revitalization of those who have made a commitment to the church. Conservation of those who have been won is as vital as winning new people. Some churches have had the experience of carrying on intensive revivals and doing little for the individual in orienting, training, and absorbing the person into the life of the church. Consequently, there is almost a procession through the church with a brief stay inside. More people may leave through the back door than are coming in the front.

The church may consciously decide in any given span of time that it will not seek aggressively for new members but will instead use the time to train the current members, not only in church responsibilities but also in what it means to be a witnessing Christian in the community. Once again, the word "witness" deserves further comment, for we are not referring here to one standing on a street corner proclaiming the Word of God. In certain situations this may have some value. But we are instead referring to the "ministry of reconciliation," where Christian men and women will look at the community and determine that a school board needs stronger members or that a community organization is in danger of foundering from lack of support. The church should honor and recognize its members who serve in community groups, giving strength and leadership to these groups as well.

When the church has recognized this phase of its ministry and built into the present membership the concept of service and of being ambassadors, it will find accessions coming. When a church looks outward, it is inevitable that citizens of the community will find vitality in this ministry and want to be a part of it.

Small churches need not be without hope or help. There are many areas of the United States, both metropolitan and nonmetropolitan, that are dependent upon a small church for its ministry.

There is an old New England saying that it is easier to move a grave than a church pew and that a lot of people don't know the difference. But, like most sayings, while it has some truth within it, it is not the whole truth. Leadership with proper vision and incentive can move churches to service, significance, and new life. Even a small church in the smallest of communities can find areas of service to meet needs and can give vital assistance to civic enterprises as well as worldwide Christian endeavor. There is a direct ratio between evangelism results in a local church and its community and world involvement through program and participation. For organizations as well as people, Jesus' words are true, that "he who would find his life must lose it for my sake."

The following code is unknown in its origin, but the value of the suggestions should not be underestimated.

A Code for the Small Church

I am one of the small churches in my state. I am not the First Church in a large city or a prosperous church in a thriving suburb.

I will respect myself. I will not indulge in self-pity because I am small.

I will develop and conserve my resources, members, and property. I will not fail to organize as I should, but I will not waste my energies in useless organization. I will organize around the ministries I must perform, thus determining that my organization shall be a means to an end.

I will not encourage factional strife of any kind: theological, denominational, or social. Other churches may be able to endure factionalism; but my resources are limited, and they must be conserved. I will endeavor to make my contribution to an intelligent, corporate decision concerning the ministries God has called us to perform. I will not knowingly be ruled by ignorance or prejudice. All attempts to fill my mind with false propaganda I will resent as an insult not to be endured.

Because I am a church, the most important fact about me is that I have a purpose and a spirit. I will minister so as to encourage all individuals to bring their lives under the lordship of Jesus Christ and to keep their spirits and purposes free from evil and full of righteousness and good will.

I recognize that the laborer, businessman, widow, child, the wealthy, and the poor man are basic in my community. Were it not for these I would have no reason to exist. I will not minister to one at the expense or neglect of any of the others.

I am a small church but I do not need to be isolated or provincial. The world is the field and it is mine to serve. As I take shape and form around the needs of the world, I am both nurtured and am able to feed others. I will not take more than I give. I will be worthy of the task God has given me and true to the hope that the world has in me because I offer the only source of the abiding satisfactions of this life and life eternal.

When the journey is long, the obstacles seem to be many, support is not immediately at hand, and the temptation is to surrender. However, in all denominations there is a rising tide of concern and a growing field of knowledge for the small church.

The initial step lies with the lay persons of the local church. If they are not concerned and are unwilling to move, then little can be done. If, on the other hand, they are interested and are ready to venture forth, testing the current practices and readjusting those practices to meet new needs, then there is no limit to the small church. It may increase in size to the extent that it will no longer be a small church. It may be noted for the significant vehicle that it is in the redemption, not only of the individual but of its community as well.

If there is the courage to be small, then the small church can find its place of ministry and its service in the kingdom that will be as meaningful in the course of time and in the history of the Christian faith as any other church unit. The work is there to be done. It can be done by no other group than the church, with its motivation of service and unselfish concern in the name of Christ. Now is the time to begin.

There are "growing points" for all churches.

Chapter

5

MUTUAL RESPONSIBILITIES

Are small churches really wanted? It will not be sufficient if this question is answered solely by denominational officials, nor will it be sufficient if this is answered by churches both large and small. It must be specifically answered by individual members of small churches. Until the individual members of small churches recognize needs and appeal for spiritual and physical support, the more remote groups can do little but wait. An offer of help by "outsiders" is not only patronizing but also is often resisted when that help is not necessarily wanted or even recognized as being needed.

The answer will still remain incomplete if it is answered by these various groups meeting individually, for the answer must be based upon mutual agreements with a partnership in mission. It will take definition of terms, plus examination of the implications of both the question and answer. Then, when there is mutual understanding, the next steps will have already been outlined in some measure. Trust, which is all too often lacking, will become a welcome by-product. If this question about the real desire for small churches could become the focal point for regional, state, and national gatherings, on both a denominational and interdenominational level, it would be extremely meaningful for the next thirty to forty years of church work.

Do we really want small churches? If the answer is "yes" (and is there really any other choice?), time is critical. The wait has been long. Habit has increased. Bewilderment and frustration have set in. Some are ready to surrender and admit defeat. Planning must take place now, for many of these churches are in such severe difficulties that it is problematical if they can be saved. The financial situation, the leadership problem, the geographical location, and the inadequate buildings have combined to such a degree that it will be only by Herculean effort and determined energies that some will be saved for a continuing ministry. The decision of the Presbyterian Church, U.S., to give priority consideration to this concern is to be commended and should be imitated by other denominations.

A primary part of the answer to the question stated above is to recognize that the task of the small church is not to produce people to fill empty pews, as valid as that is. The primary purpose of any church, large or small, must be service in the name of God, accomplishing that service through a complete program of teaching, worship, community outreach, and fellowship. Simply to seek for people is selfish. To seek for people that their lives may be enriched and changed is a totally different purpose. Pews can be full, but churches can still be sterile and empty of significance if there is no vision of mission and commitment to that mission.

Small churches do have a ministry that is vital, and that can be exciting to themselves and to the communities they serve. They can have comprehensive ministries as well, serving all ages and needs, though the denominational format and structure may not necessarily be followed. There must be carved out a special niche and place for the ministry of the small church based upon research and agreement on long-range plans and procedures. It must originate with the denomination, for the small church in and of itself is too weak, too lacking in connection with others in a similar plight to be able to begin on the task.

There is evidence that the denominations care and are concerned. However, far too little has been done to implement the knowledge that has been developed. The population explosion, the many new suburban communities with high potential, and the demands for radical ministries in the urban areas all combine to command the focus of attention. Too little time and energy is left for the churches that may desperately need help but which have been on the scene for so long that they are accepted as a kind of querulous maiden aunt who has problems but has always had problems and, therefore, is not as deserving of attention as the new infant who has been in the world only a short time. Lay persons may hold the answer to such erratic procedure. Churches in similar situations can counsel together and then solicit denominational help. Interested men and women can request relevant materials, with qualified personnel to interpret. Until the people of the local churches, however, show some evidence of knowledge of their plight and their willingness to move, progress will continue to be of a limping nature. In some few areas such movements have begun. Other areas and regions must also begin. The denomination will have to be prepared to give as much support in planning, finances, and staff attention to the small church as it has to other churches of high potential. There will have to be a modification of denominational programs so that the small church will not have to be constantly adapting materials to fit its needs, thereby compounding its guilt feelings. In fact, wholly new materials may be demanded especially for these churches.

There will also have to be an acceptance by the churches that historically the Christian faith has been one of cooperation and interdependence. "States' rights" have little place in the kingdom. There must be a recognition of the unity that comes in Christ. If strategy indicates that a local church should change its ministry or even close its doors, there should be a calm acceptance that the kingdom of God demands sacrifice and the willingness to lose our lives that others might find it.

The federal government has expressed its concern for what it calls "core cities." These are communities that, because of location, access to resources, and labor and market potentials, must be strengthened. There are "core churches," too, that are essential for denominational and interdenominational strategy. Losing them would be catastrophic. Some may now be "small churches" and will continue to be so. They may be in a county seat, in the heart of a city on a central shopping square, or at a place of influence where the Christian witness is imperative. But, wherever they are, "core churches" must be identified and supported to full and vital life. This may require task forces of denominational staff who understand community organization and development as well as Christian goals and denominational programs. These task forces must go to the point of need and meet the problem, remaining until there is order and progress once again implicit in the situation. Not all local needs have the same elements in the same intensity and the same frequency. To expect local people to understand the dynamics and to be able to analyze a situation is unfair and unrealistic. It has taken years of training for denominational staff to have this skill.

Denominational program goals may need to be put into a secondary priority for a period of time that staff persons may begin at the point of need in a local situation. If program is temporarily subordinated to giving this assistance in a local situation, then program takes its rightful place, which is providing the tools to a strong laborer ready for the task. Too often, literature of denominations gives the appearance that programs are ends. They must be means. A program that is completely followed and faithfully executed may have little lasting impact, for it may not speak to the individual needs of a particular area at a specific time. Our nation does have regional differences, such as the South, New England, the Great Plains, and others. Some of these differences are being accentuated with population mobility, urban growth, industrialization, and changes in occupational status of millions. Small churches are particularly vulnerable to these differences. Task forces would give incentive, interpretation in change, and provide opportunity for a vital response.

This approach sounds expensive, and it could be, although it does not have to be. The tragedy is that many of the dollars now being used in small churches are being used inefficiently and are securing far fewer results than dollars used in the same way in larger situations. The human cost cannot be calculated, but any pastor of a small church can tell of the discouragement that all too frequently exists. For adults this problem is critical; but far more serious is that numbers of young people have drifted away because the small church too often is not capable of challenging them and then sustaining that challenge.

There may be modifications of buildings, the development of new tools for education and evangelism, and new forms of ministry that would result from such attention. There would be a substantial fringe benefit. Many local, denominational staff people confirm the fact that the majority of their time is now spent in assisting small churches merely maintain life with very little time being given in program help, community outreach, and service. Under present circumstances, it is a vicious cycle that has to be repeated at short intervals because of changes in pastoral leadership.

There is a tension that frequently exists between local churches and their respective denominations. The small church is often conservative, not only in theology, but also in its action patterns and sociological stance. It is likely to judge its own activities by criteria developed from faith and history. If services of worship are held and there is a church school, with occasional church dinners, some feel that it constitutes a church, for these are the most observable characteristics of a church. The form is there, and the question may remain unanswered as to whether change is taking place in those who are in attendance. The denomination, on the other hand, concerned for finances, church placement, and wise and proper use of ministerial leadership, is far more pragmatic in its approach and looks at action and results. It looks at statistical tables of accessions, of giving, and of participation. Frequently such tables are made up in such a way that they do not indicate ratios but simply totals. Totals are frequently injurious to the small church, for they are not put in proper relationship with the base from which they came. The denomination is more likely to take its criteria from environment and the pattern of institutionalism.

Both standards are valid standards and both must be used. Faith and action are twins in Christian theology and mission. The local church must, however, move toward the criteria of action, and the denomination must temper its judgments with criteria of faith. It is never a clear case of one or the other. Jesus said, "where two or three are gathered. . . ." This was a clear recognition of the standards of faith. No man wanting a ministry can be deserted. The parable of the good Samaritan is clear as a criterion of action.

The test of the Christian faith is not efficiency. Actually, statistical studies that go further than simply looking at total figures provide a good case for the work of the small church. Churches in this category average one and a half to two times more the attendance at worship in relationship to membership than does a large church. Small churches give more on a per capita basis than do members of large churches. Admittedly, much of the giving of members of small churches goes into the local church for maintenance rather than mission, but the studies still reveal that individual members do give more. When figures for church accessions are worked out, again the small church figures are often better than those of large churches.

There is a logical partnership, therefore, of small churches, larger churches, and denominations, as well as interdenominational bodies. Each has a place and each has a contribution. None can be ignored.

The Denomination Owes the Church

Assumptions are made easily. We meet a few persons, visit with them, and come to the conclusion that "everyone" thinks as these do. But assumptions need to be examined and tested on occasion to be certain that they are valid.

What is the most typical size of the churches of a particular denomination? For whom does the denomination prepare its programs? It is a fascinating exercise to be in a church group and ask these questions. It becomes quickly apparent that there are varying ideas of the typical size of a church. The debate concerning for whom programs are prepared is even sharper, for emotions and frustrations are apt to enter in at this point. Yet these two questions are so important that subjective judgments should not be permitted. It is fairly easy to determine specific, concrete answers to these questions. They do not need to be questions of judgment as they are so often. They can be facts. They should be facts. Planning groups may assume the average size of a church to be five hundred, for example. One half of the churches may have less than two hundred members. Both statements may be true, for the number of quite large churches may push the average membership up. It still remains, however, that the largest portion of churches are "small." Does the denomination then program for the "average" church though the majority are small, or does it temper its program by recognizing the numbers of churches in various categories? Obviously the answer leads to quite different conclusions and very different planning and programming.

For the sake of the spiritual health of the small church and for the energies of the denomination, precise answers need to be reached. It is too costly to be always preparing programs, training staff, and enlisting volunteer leaders for programs that cannot be used by small churches. Goals must be set that are realistic in the light of the total needs of the denomination. The denomination, therefore, owes to each church, large or small, as vital a program as can be conceived and used with a minimum of adaptation. If there is to be adaptation, let it be in the large church where more creative resources are available.

There needs to be a centralized planning body within each denomination that not only looks at programs that are being planned but also charts the committees that will be needed. Program coordination is not unusual these days in denominations. Calendars are prepared in order that there will be as little competition for time and as little duplication of effort as possible. But too seldom is there a projection to the local church level of what the newest program means to the local congregation in committee structure when it is piled on top of an already overloaded structure. A denomination has a responsibility to determine the basic program that is expected of each church and the basic budget that will be essential to meet that program. If such studies clearly indicate that a large percentage of churches just cannot fulfill the plans, then it is obvious that the planning group needs to reconsider and become more realistic. It will probably never be possible to include all of the churches in any one program, for the common denominator would be so low that there would be no challenge. However, plans that are prepared on a national level must be carefully projected into representative churches of the denomination to determine their feasibility. This cannot be done on "hearsay" evidence of casual committees. In the day in which we live it is possible to measure almost anything. Certainly the church of Christ should be using the finest of tools, for its task is a holy one. Realistic planning has no substitute, and review and evaluation must be a part of the process.

Financial Help

In the instance of a small church which is essential to denominational strategy, it is almost a foregone conclusion that denominational subsidy will be needed in some fashion. By tradition, this subsidy is usually at the point of the pastor's salary. Such a subsidy is inadequate, however, if it has only this one dimension. Enlarged vision on the part of key lay persons might make unnecessary the subsidy for a pastor's salary. Scholarships for short-term courses at conferences for the laity could be more meaningful, for a revitalized laity means a revitalized church. Subsidy in the form of Christian education materials, with the loan of a qualified staff instructor in the use of the materials, might be better stewardship in terms of long-term results.

If the small church is to receive help, two principles should be involved. The help should have limits stipulated and agreed upon in advance (barring unforeseen circumstances) in order that the church does not become dependent upon this source of income. The help should lead to self-respect and dignity for the local congregation. The second principle is ascertaining the purpose of the financial support. Put in its basic language, support buys time. But for what purpose? Is it simply to prolong the life of a church that may be dying and has little chance of coming alive again because of community conditions? This goal is hardly Christian. Is the support given to undergird a program that is vital and does have a place but requires short-term investment by the denomination? Denominational help should be given to strengthen churches, not to perpetuate weakness. Frequently the members of a church have one objective in view, but the denominational staff has another viewpoint. All too often, these different objectives are not revealed until a time of crisis some years later. There should be discussion and agreement upon objectives at the very beginning; otherwise, cooperation does not really exist and the support given will fail to have any long lasting results.

If denominational support is given to the pastor's salary, then the denomination has an obligation to encourage the pastor to stay long enough to be effective. A short-term pastor cannot accomplish the essential goals. Some things may be done and done well. The ground may be prepared for someone who comes later, but the one who comes next may not accept the same priorities. Momentum is also lost in any change of pastorates. The salary must be adequate. The living accommodations must be satisfactory. There must be care that there are proper allowances for the car used in church work, for continuing education, and for other areas that ultimately are for the benefit of the church, though at first they may appear to be for the minister. The denomination needs, in its own way, to pay tribute to those who conscientiously labor upon the "small fields" and to give them honor and recognition. Usually recognition given by the denomination is to the pastor who serves in a large church that is influential and is a prestige church. One must ask the purpose of such honor. Is it simply to recognize success, or is it to recognize ability, dedication, and faithfulness? These attributes are often found in small fields, too, particularly where denominations have encouraged pastors to be career persons in specialized areas. The answers to these and kindred questions may lead to a revision in the choice of those who are recognized, honored, and invited to share in committee and denominational life. It is not true to say that in all instances the pastor who is in a large church is without question the best of the denomination. There are others, equally able, who have experienced a call to a particular type of field or who for other reasons feel a commitment to a different area of service.

Participation

The denomination has a responsibility to make room for participation not only by ministers of smaller churches but also by the laity. Larger churches usually give more than twice as much on a dollar basis as smaller churches to the general work of the denomination. A major reason for this is that there are irreducible minimums in the operation of any building and organization. The small churches simply do not have the same amount left for the wider interests.

Having said that, however, it is often true that denominations have a tendency to make speakers available and to provide more promotional helps in large churches. Small churches could and would give more if they had more adequate help in interpretation, promotion of denominational programs, and support that leads to a greater involvement.

Brains are not a monopoly of the members of the large church. People for personal reasons often elect a different style of living or a different type of community. They may prefer a small church. If they have a contribution to make, they have the right to expect that the denomination will examine its processes and be certain that there is a balance of voices, interests, and concerns. One of the historic principles of our nation is that every person has a right to be heard. In church life this is true as well. All sections of denominational life have a right to expect that they will be represented when policies are developed and programs are established.

Psychologists have developed "attitudinal studies" that reveal how individuals feel about various proposals and ideas. Such a sampling of opinion needs to be a part of the regular pattern of each denomination. Decisions may or may not be different. There will be, however, a sense of sharing that is vital, particularly if the previous methods have not involved all groups. Regardless of the method, care must be exercised that the attitudes are understood. Responsible leadership always reserves the right to proceed in a direction different from that desired by their constituents, for other facts may be known to leadership that are less apparent to constituency. This is a responsibility of leadership. However, each person and each church in the denomination has a right to respect, dignity, a feeling of participation, and a sense of understanding and being understood. It is easy at a store counter to let a small child be shoved aside while the adults are served by the clerk. A small church can also be pushed aside at critical times when it is seeking to be heard. A child will not always return when he has received such treatment. Neither will a small church. The author has heard too often in small churches about the times they had tried to secure help, speakers, or guidance and had been refused. They had not tried the same source again. In churches with congregational government this has often been the first move away from the denomination. The feeling of not wanting the small church may not have been in the mind of the denomination, but the small church may have thought it was. The church is not helped to overcome such an attitude by a denial by the denomination.

Life Expectancy

The church of Jesus Christ in considered to be eternal. Local congregations, however, are not. There are changes. There are new needs. There are movements of people that change ministries. Do churches have a "life expectancy" as people do that can be calculated with actuarial accuracy? The answer must be a qualified "yes." Many denominations now have research sections that are growing increasingly competent in their ability to predict patterns of growth and change in specific situations. There are still errors in the process. The human factors, too, of lay and ministerial leadership keep the results from being 100 percent accurate. Yet, with astonishing accuracy, it can be determined whether a church will continue at its present level, whether it has an opportunity to grow, or whether it will be forced to decline because of external factors. There are spiritual factors that also need to be applied to the life of an individual church.

Change is not defeat unless a church chooses to make it so. As a matter of fact, people outside a particular church are often more aware of the significance of change than the people who are inside the church. Faithfulness in service is more critical than length of life. The accomplishments of Jesus are not measured by the length of his life but rather by the quality of his life and his death as well.

A denomination needs to place constantly before its member churches the concept of service. It needs to have a strategy of placement that recognizes the "population explosion" as well as the need of ministry in areas of declining population. To maintain all existing churches simply because they exist is foolish. However, no denomination has a right to withdraw its support and identification from a small church without first being certain that the spiritual needs will be met.

Those needs may not always be met in exactly the same fashion or even perhaps by the same denomination. There can be ecumenical planning that will mean the continuance of one church, ministering to the people who were formerly affiliated with several churches.

A critical factor in life expectancy is in the type of ministerial leadership which is provided. Too often the small church is at one end or the other of the years of a minister's life. It either has a minister who is vigorous but lacking in experience or one who is wise in experience but lacking in vigor. There are definite exceptions, but rarely does a small church have a minister who is at the maximum peak of both wisdom and energy in the years of service. A denomination owes the best of leadership to the church that is being hurt seriously. If the best is not currently available, then training is essential so that those who are now in such positions may be numbered among the "best" eventually. If such denominational help is given, then the pastor has an obligation to stay in the small church, using the training for the purpose for which it was intended.

The Church Owes the Denomination

Regardless of the polity of a particular denomination, it is possible for a church to participate fully or "to drag its feet." Churches that are capable of doing a great deal sometimes do far less for either a real or an imagined reason. This is always regrettable, for churches suffer, members are hurt, and the total Christian cause is affected as people outside the church look at the internal dissensions. Such situations should not be tolerated if there are any possible solutions. A local church does owe its denomination the recognition of history, tradition, and the loyalty that grows out of such recognition. There may be temporary reasons for disturbance, but these should be more than counterbalanced by recognizing the decades of affiliation.

Little has been said about those places where there is emotional tension, pique, and division. Small churches can be victims of individuals who are personally upset and have become vocal. Out of courtesy, there may be no active questioning or opposition. Such a personal attitude can become cancerous and spread into the total organism. Denominational staff are often willing to move into such a situation to help but have no invitation, even if they are aware of the need. Local congregations become offended because no one is answering their questions. Who breaks the ice and makes the first approach? How are problems handled when a church is upset for whatever reason? Several denominations are now experimenting by dealing with specialists in organizational development who are professionally trained to deal with tension and interpersonal relationships. There must be openness to such a process, obviously, but this approach to problem solving can prove to be most fruitful to the local congregation.

There are very few churches of any denomination west of the Mississippi that did not have denominational help to a large degree in their beginning. This is true to a lesser degree of churches east of the Mississippi, but, even there a very large proportion of churches received not only funds for building but also support for program in the beginning.

There has been less visible support that has continued as well. Many denominational publications require some subsidy from the budget of the denomination. Even if there is no subsidy, few churches pay the actual cost of the materials that they use, for there is a sharing of writing fees and production costs that is covered in volume which no single church could cover. Denominational staff is employed for specific program functions. These services are usually available to local churches without any charge or in specialized services with only a minimum payment. Services of denominational staff are often accepted without thought or recognition of the denomination's concern. Many denominations have competent, highly trained specialists at the state or area level to assist the local congregation. There are common services established for the benefit of all, such as camps, conference grounds, educational institutions, and other such facilities. Some denominations have insurance programs for employees in local churches. All of these had their origins in denominational budgets and may still be drawing upon such resources. Certainly all are based on mass buying power with decreased cost to individual participants. Churches are not able to function alone. The church owes the denomination recognition for these resources, and the local church needs to accept these as being a part of life. There need not be any feeling of undue loyalty because of them, but neither can there in good conscience be a minimizing of what these resources have meant over the years.

There is mutuality.

The Fetish of Autonomy

Local churches often make a great deal of the fact that they have local rights that supersede all other claims. In some instances, these are just claims and the rights are significant. However, to pursue this course too far is neither logical nor fair. As has been pointed out, churches cannot exist alone. No church that has a minister has paid the cost of the training of that minister. Seminaries train students with funds that come from individuals, from legacies, and from the general budget of the denomination. Any church that has a pastor is "in debt" to the denomination for training the person who is now leading them. Local rights, if emphasized too much, are not fair to the church universal. We are accustomed as individuals to obeying traffic signals which may cause us considerable inconvenience in our personal schedules, but we do this in recognition of the "common good."

There is a "common good" for churches as well. Not all churches will benefit equally at the same time, but schedules and programs must be developed with the greatest value for all. Some individual churches may find less value in a specific instance or even considerable difficulty in adjusting, but this is a part of being in society. An individual citizen may never make use of the fire equipment in his community, but what citizen fails to appreciate its availability? Local churches need to recognize that they make limited use of some resources of denominational life but that, if these resources are needed elsewhere, there is obvious value for the aggregate welfare of all.

It is impossible to "go it alone" in today's society. This has never been possible theologically, for Jesus emphasized community of interest and need. It is not possible to live alone physically, for groceries, hardware stores, and other such facilities are established only where there are groups. John Donne's poem with the phrase "No man is an island" has become almost a cliché. Literature and drama are filled with stories of men and women who could not exist alone. The local church must recognize that even though it may claim autonomy it is deceiving itself. If that local congregation can produce its own teaching materials, its own ministers, train its laity, and do everything for itself without recourse to the outside, only then can it claim to be autonomous.

Actually, the argument for autonomy which is pursued by so many local churches is an evasion of responsibility. Local churches have put forth the concept that they live "apart from" others. Christian theology says the local church is to be "a part of" the world. Jesus was bitterly condemned in his day for those with whom he associated. He did not always choose the righteous people of the community, but he found the people with needs, even though sometimes these people were on the fringes of respectable society. The church of today must be a part of life as well, ministering to people with needs. Respectability may be desirable, but it is not always the key to ministry.

The church owes the denomination the reconsideration of the parish concept. Even in the so-called "free churches," where the concept of parish is not well developed, there are parishes. A parish may not be geographical, for a church may minister to a cultural or language group, or to a class in society. A church may be limiting its own ministry and growth by accepting the boundaries which it has placed for itself over the years. This may have been a valid ministry. The question must be raised about the present, however. In our highly mobile society there may still be reasons for a minority language-group church to exist. However, the need is almost extinct in the United States today with the possible exception of the Hispanic population. If a church is in this category, it needs to be careful, for it may be denying to its members and particularly its youth the full range of human fellowship as well as denying the range of the gospel. Staff time will be needed from the denomination to assist the church in this evaluation, but most denominations not only have the staff, but are also most eager for such opportunities. A great deal of ferment is taking place currently concerning the limited viewpoints and services of many local churches and of their need to gain a new vision. Resources are available and the local church has a responsibility to use these resources.

Some of the resources or programs at first may appear to be of dubious value or interest. Actually, they may be far more meaningful when once begun than could have been anticipated. In the freshness of approach and in the new dimension of life, individual church members may find help for their own personal living as well as new stimuli. An unvarying diet of beans becomes monotonous rather quickly. The diet can be helped by the addition of bacon and some vegetables. But beans are even better when they are on the table occasionally, with other things on the menu in between. A church program needs variety, too. Individual church members need variety. A church sometimes needs to enter into new areas or program for the increased zest that may be given to the church life.

There are times, of course, when there will be local needs that will not be met by denominational programs that are being offered. Prodding of the denomination is to be encouraged on those occasions. There may be no immediate results, but what is felt by one church may be a need in another church as well that has not been indicated. Continued lifting up of concerns may stimulate action. A church which has a keen need has a responsibility to let the denomination know about it.

The church owes the denomination financial support. The local church often receives many helps for which it never pays. These come from the general budget of the denomination and are a part of the total mission. If direct support or help comes, the local church needs to understand the terms of that support. It needs also to recognize that "bargaining" may have to take place. This is not because denominational staff wants it that way or is trying to evade responsibility but because there is a "trust obligation." When money is given by many hundreds of churches into a general budget, there have to be general policies. While these can be varied somewhat in local situations, they still must be followed with some degree of faithfulness. A local church has a responsibility not to ask for other than that which it truly needs to be faithful in mission and to lend its strength to the task which is at hand.

Ecumenical Responsibility

While the bulk of this chapter has centered upon the individual church and its denomination, the interdenominational aspects cannot be overlooked or minimized.

One of the weaknesses of ecumenical work thus far has been its inability to implement on a local level what has been worked out and proclaimed on an international or national level. There can be a meeting of the minds in work groups in the National Council of Churches or other ecumenical groups with rather detailed proposals developed. There is no binding force, however, in implementation. Some denominations are even unable to interpret adequately to the local constituency the meaning of actions that were taken.

There have been significant conferences on a state or multi-state basis in some instances. In Alaska, under the auspices of the Alaska Council of Churches, very valuable steps have been taken to develop a statewide approach to the churching of Alaska. Over a period of years, there have been conferences on sparsely settled areas primarily centering in Colorado, Wyoming, Montana, and the Dakotas. While these have been educational and beneficial, there has been little specific implementation at the local level. Some new communities have sought to develop a new strategy for churching, with a notable instance being Howard County in Maryland.

By and large, much more needs to be done to assist denominations and local churches to implement interdenominational cooperation in the many villages, towns, and cities of our nation. To enforce cooperation is obviously a contradiction in terms. Cooperation must come out of a feeling of need and a desire to achieve a better way of accomplishing the objectives and goals.

The word "comity" has fallen into disrepute because of abuse of the principle within some ecclesiastical groups and the ignoring of it by others. "Adjustment procedures" have come into vogue but have been of little more value. There may be assignment to a particular denomination of the responsibility for the maintenance of a Christian witness within a given area. However, if the area becomes one of high potential, it is amazing to discover how many reasons can be found to discard agreements that were laboriously established a short time ago. Denominations have an obligation to local churches to arrive at better methods for churching villages and towns and cities. Local churches have a responsibility to denominations to be more open-minded in listening to proposals and the reasons for those proposals. Not all such proposals originate in the desire of a denominational official to prove that he is busy. Some have valid objectives, arrived at after years of experience, that would permit a better servicing of the community in the name of Christ and with better stewardship involved.

The World Council of Churches has engaged in a study on the missionary structure of the congregation. It is obvious that the present church organizational pattern has become so freighted with superfluous committees that time and energy needed for other pursuits are being frittered away. There is no clear evidence of a better pattern, but movements are taking place that will permit the churches to reach out in evangelism and social issues. Much of the current church structure is a remnant of history rather than a tool for mission. Lay persons in local churches need to look at how they are being asked to use their time and energy and for what purpose.

The solutions for small church problems do not lie in more money, more people, and more leaders, though all of these are obviously beneficial. Planning, the establishment of realistic goals, and a renewed sense of mission are the answers to the problems.

The small church needs to remember its assets rather than its liabilities. The small church must carefully study the issues that are involved and recognize that it may have to sacrifice breadth of program for depth. The small church may have to accept the fact that physical growth is limited because of the nature of its community, but its opportunity for spiritual growth and service is unlimited. People have needs. Those needs must be met. The church of Jesus Christ has unique gifts, assets, and insights to bring to the task. In service and surrender to service, the small church will find its life and thus find itself.